D1351293

Handbook of Trout and Salmon Diseases

Handbook of Trout and Salmon Diseases

by

Ronald J Roberts

PhD BVMS MRCPath MRCVS FRSE

University of Stirling

and

C Jonathan Shepherd

PhD MSc BVSc MRCVS

Marine Harvest Limited

Fishing News Books Ltd
Farnham, Surrey, England

Reprint 1979

Unit of Aquatic Pathobiology
University of Stirling
Scotland

ISBN 0 85238 066 6

Printed in Great Britain by
The Whitefriars Press Ltd, London and Tonbridge

List of Contents

		page
Preface		7
Acknowledgements		9
List of Figures		11
List of Tables		13
Frontispiece		15
Chapter I	The Cultured Salmonids	17
Chapter II	The Anatomy of Salmonid Fish	22
Chapter III	Husbandry of Salmonid Fish	34
Chapter IV	Infectious Diseases	43
Chapter V	Disease Diagnosis on the Farm	76
Chapter VI	Diseases of Eggs and Sac-Fry (Alevins)	81
Chapter VII	Diseases of Early Feeding	87
Chapter VIII	Diseases of Growers	94
Chapter IX	Diseases of Marine Culture	118
Chapter X	Nutritional Diseases	124
Chapter XI	Fish Kills	129
Chapter XII	Diseases of Wild Fish and Broodstock	131
Chapter XIII	Prevention and Treatment of Disease	144
Appendices		160
Index		165

Preface

This handbook is intended for the practical trout and salmon hatcheryman, fish farmer, angler, and resource manager. It was originally conceived as an adjunct to the short courses provided by the Aquatic Pathobiology Unit of the University of Stirling.

In the original form it was written in conjunction with Dr E A Needham and Mr C W Poupard, of Unilever Research (Colworth/Welwyn Laboratory), Aberdeen, and we gratefully acknowledge their help and assistance both with the original manual and with this expanded volume.

No attempt has been made to use scientific names if commonly used names give a more easily understood, if less exact, meaning. Also, although the conditions discussed are of major significance in our present experience, there is no suggestion that they are the only diseases to affect salmonids or that subsequent experience will not force us to reconsider our ideas as to what is and is not an important disease.

It is the belief of the authors that most of the disease problems described in this book can be largely prevented by a combination of good husbandry and specific precautions on the farm. If this is true, then the more the fish farmer understands about the possibility of disease among his stock, the greater should be his ability to cut down on losses from diseases and so operate more profitably.

Acknowledgements

In addition to the comprehensive assistance of Dr Needham and Mr Poupard[8] detailed in the preface, we would like to thank various friends and colleagues for the time and trouble which they spent in correcting and improving the text and in providing photographs of disease conditions; in particular we would mention the following: Mr F Bregnballe,[4] Prof N O Christensen, Denmark; Dr R Bootsma, Holland; Dr T Kimura, Japan; Dr T Håstein, Norway; Mr C H Aldridge,[2] Dr J I W Anderson, Dr J S Buchanan, Mr D Bucke, Dr B J Hill,[1] Dr M Halliday, Dr L M Laird, Mr J F McArdle, Dr K MacKenzie, Mr W M Shearer, Dr C Sommerville, UK, Dr L N Allison, Dr G L Hoffman, Prof G W Klontz, Dr J D Larmoyeux, Mr J C Lientz, Dr F P Meyer,[3,5,6] Dr R R Rucker, Dr C E Smith,[7] Dr S F Snieszko, Mr W T Yasutake, Dr K E Wolf, Prof R D Wolke, USA; Dr M von Lukowicz, West Germany. Further acknowledgement to the work of six of these individuals is made (in chapter XIII) by the use of superscript numbers corresponding to the small numbers given above.

This handbook represents part of the educational programme in fish diseases and husbandry at the Unit of Aquatic Pathobiology, University of Stirling, Scotland. The Unit was established by the Nuffield Foundation and is also supported by the Wellcome Trust, The Natural Environment Research Council, and The Atlantic Salmon Research Trust; we are pleased to acknowledge these organizations. Special thanks are due to Mrs Elsie Kirk for typing the manuscripts with such patience; also to Mr R B Stewart, Mrs M Stevenson and Mr G McCue, of the audiovisual aids unit at Stirling University for help with photographic material and to Mrs Helen Roberts for line drawings.

List of Figures

page

Fig 1 Line drawing: Anatomy of Salmon   23
Fig 2 (a, b, c, d) Scales: parr and adult   25
Fig 3 Gills/Rakers and Operculum   26
Fig 4 Heart   27
Fig 5 Digestive system   28
Fig 6 Swim bladder   30
Fig 7 Brain   32
Fig 8 Table of Salmonid Parasites   44
Fig 9 (a, b, c, d) *Costia*   46, 47
Fig 10 *Henneguya*   48
Fig 11 (a) *Ichthyophthirius* (b) *Trichodina* (c) Blue
       sac (d) Furunculosis   15, 16
Fig 12 (a) Two host stages of *Ichthyophthirius* in skin
       (b) Life cycle of *Ichthyophthirius*   49
Fig 13 Whirling disease   50
Fig 14 *Hexamita* and gut cells   51
Fig 15 *Oodinium*   52
Fig 16 *Scyphidia* complex   53
Fig 17 *Chilodonella*   53
Fig 18 *Acanthocephalus*   54
Fig 19 *Eubothrium*   56
Fig 20 *Argulus*   58
Fig 21 *Lernaea*   58
Fig 22 *Lepeophtheirus*   59
Fig 23 *Salmincola*   59
Fig 24 *Anisakis*   60
Fig 25 *Gyrodactylus*   61
Fig 26 Life cycle: *Cryptocotyle*   62
Fig 27 Cercaria of *Cryptocotyle*   63
Fig 28 Life cycle: *Diplostomum*   64
Fig 29 *Diplostomum*: smear of macerated lens   65
Fig 30 Lamprey   66
Fig 31 Leech   66
Fig 32 *Glochidia*   67
Fig 33 *Flexibacter*   71
Fig 34 *Cytophaga*   71

Fig 35 (a, b) *Ichthyophonus*   page 74
Fig 36 *Saprolegnia*   75
Fig 37 *Scolecobasidium*   75
Fig 38 Stages in preparing a wet-mount   78
Fig 39 Eyed Eggs   82
Fig 40 Siamese twins   83
Fig 41 Deformed yolk sac   84
Fig 42 (a) Gas bubble disease in sac fry (b) Gas
        bubble disease in gills   85
Fig 43 Starved salmon pinheads   87
Fig 44 IPN   89
Fig 45 VHS. Acute haemorrhage on testis   98
Fig 46 Chronic VHS. Black colour and popeye   99
Fig 47 Chronic VHS (post-mortem)   99
Fig 48 IHN   101
Fig 49 Whirling disease   103
Fig 50 Ich on salmon parr   104
Fig 51 External parasitism (mild lesion)   106
Fig 52 Bald spot   108
Fig 53 Fin rot   109
Fig 54 Peduncle disease   110
Fig 55 Eye showing Eye Fluke   112
Fig 56 Lens with Eye Fluke   112
Fig 57 *Nocardia* infection   113
Fig 58 *Nocardia* (post-mortem)   113
Fig 59 BKD (Kidney)   114
Fig 60 BKD (Muscle)   115
Fig 61 PKD (Kidney)   116
Fig 62 'Bad-doer'   116
Fig 63 Vibriosis (post-mortem)   119
Fig 64 Sea lice on salmon head   121
Fig 65 Cold water disease   122
Fig 66 Skeletal fry   125
Fig 67 Fatty liver   127
Fig 68 Skin fungus   133
Fig 69 Autumn Aeromonad disease   134
Fig 70 (a, b, c, d) UDN   137, 138
Fig 71 Thymic tumour   139
Fig 72 Malignant tumour on jaw   139
Fig 73 Gills showing gill maggots   141
Fig 74 Acanthocephalans attached to gut   143
Fig 75 *Triaenophorus*   143
Fig 76 Microscope   161

12

List of Tables

		page
1	Differentiation between *S. salar* and *S. trutta*	20
2	The Salmonidae	21
3	Significant Pathogenic Bacteria	68
4	Diagnostic Signs of Disease among Growers	96, 97
5	Conversion Factors	147
6	Medicated Food Calculation Tables	157
7	Trout Diseases—Useful Drugs and Chemicals	164
8	Salmonid Parasites (fig 8)	44

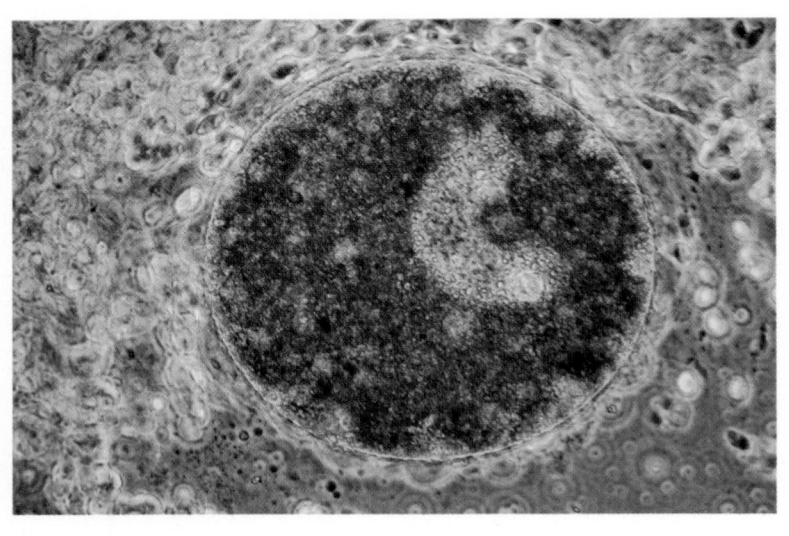

Fig 11   Frontispiece. (a) *Ichthyophthirius multifiliis*. This illustration shows the adult stage of this parasite with its characteristic horseshoe-shaped nucleus. It is usually brown coloured and revolves slowly. It is approximately 0.5 mm in size and may be seen in skin scrapings under low   power   magnification.

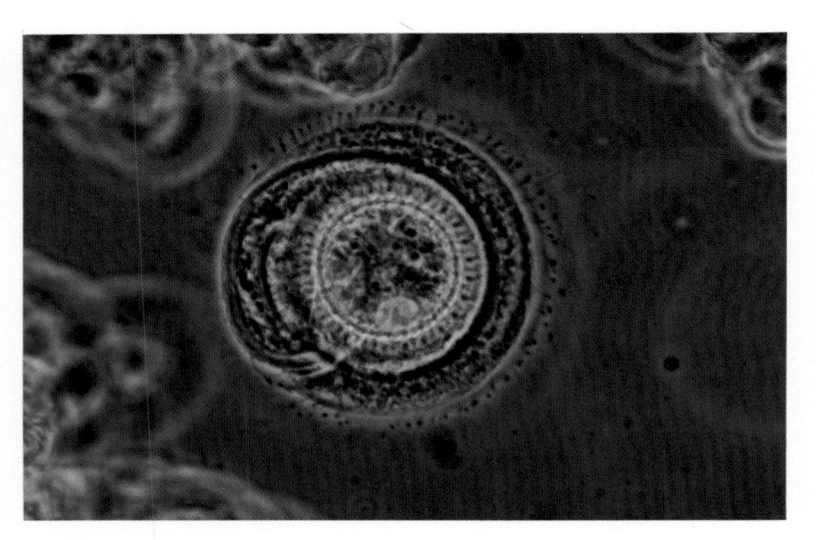

(b) *Trichodina*. This parasite, with its saw-toothed structure, revolves very slowly and is readily seen under low power in gill and skin smears.

Photographs (a) and (b) by courtesy of Mr C H Aldridge.
Copyright, Unilever Research Laboratories.

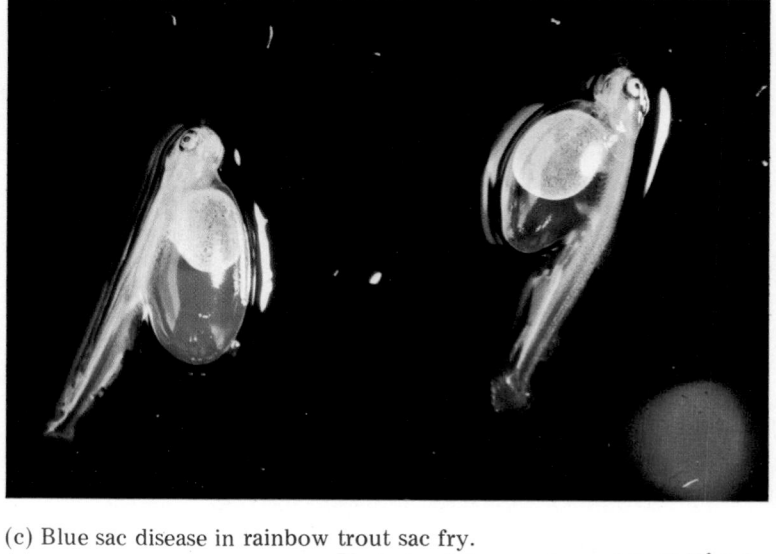

(c) Blue sac disease in rainbow trout sac fry.

Photograph by courtesy of Dr T Håstein.

(d) Furunculosis in a brown trout. This specimen shows the characteristic raised furuncles. The fish was taken in Autumn and hence the rather uncharacteristic concurrent fungus infection.

Chapter I The Cultured Salmonids

The farming or culture of fish under controlled conditions, has been practised for thousands of years but the farming of salmonid fish — the salmon and trout groups — is a fairly recent activity. Salmon and trout were first hatched and reared under artificial conditions during the last century, primarily for stocking waters for anglers, but the Danes pioneered the farming of rainbow trout (*Salmo gairdneri*) for human consumption. More recently 'table production' of rainbow trout has become popular in most continents of the world, and attempts are now being made to farm Atlantic salmon (*Salmo salar*) in Scotland and Norway, and Pacific salmon (*Oncorhynchus* spp.) in the USA and Canada. Other salmonids regularly farmed include brown trout (*Salmo trutta*) and brook trout (*Salvelinus fontinalis*) for restocking purposes.

The family *Salmonidae* is usually divided into two sub-families, the *Salmonini*, which includes all of the sport and commonly cultured species, and the *Coregonini*, which includes the whitefish or freshwater herrings (gwynniad, pollan, powan, vendace); (see Table 2).

This book is concerned solely with the *Salmonini* and when the term salmonid is used, it is as a collective noun embracing four genera; a genus being a collection of related species.

1 Genus *Salmo*

The most famous of the salmonids is the Atlantic salmon. This is closely related to the brown trout, sea trout and the rainbow trout. The young salmon is referred to as a 'parr' until it develops its silvery coat prior to migrating as a 'smolt' to sea, where it grows very rapidly on the rich food available there. Returning from sea, it is referred to as a 'grilse', if it returns after one winter at sea, and a 'salmon' if it has spent more than one winter at sea. It is often exceedingly difficult to distinguish between juvenile Atlantic salmon and brown trout, and between large sea trout and adult Atlantic salmon. Table 1 indicates the various differences but no one feature is sufficiently constant for complete reliability.

The rainbow trout is usually distinguished by its smaller spots, its smaller scales, the more abundant spotting of tail and fins, and the iridescent line down each side which is evident in certain lights.

Rainbow trout grow in freshwater, much faster than Atlantic salmon or brown trout, and so for culinary purposes are the most frequently cultured. Brown trout are almost exclusively farmed for restocking purposes. Atlantic salmon were originally reared solely up to the parr stage, to place in streams in order to increase future returning adult numbers, or to replace fish which would have hatched in nursery streams impounded for reservoir purposes. However, now they are also farmed in combined freshwater and marine facilities, for table production of adult fish.

The sea trout is considered to be identical with the brown trout — merely a brown trout which has decided to feed in the richer waters of the sea, and the steelhead is a similar form of rainbow trout. Like salmon, sea trout parr also smoltify and become silvery-coloured on going to sea. There are a number of areas where land-locked Atlantic salmon occur, and these use large lakes as their 'inland sea'. The Atlantic salmon on the Baltic are almost exclusively produced in hatcheries, mainly in Sweden, to compensate for the loss of former nursery streams to hydro-electricity production or factory use.

2 Genus *Oncorhynchus* The Pacific salmon

The Pacific salmon are found in the rivers of most Pacific coasts, both East and West. In addition, they are sometimes found in Atlantic salmon fisheries, as a result of transplantations made from Russian Pacific Waters to North-west Russian Arctic Ocean/Atlantic Waters.

The generic name of the Pacific salmon is *Oncorhynchus*, meaning hooked nose, which refers to the very marked hooked nose and kype possessed by most of the males at spawning. The duration of the different stages of the life cycle of Pacific salmon is more constant than that of the

Atlantic salmon, and all Pacific salmon die after spawning.

The biggest of all the salmon, the king salmon, quinnat, or chinook salmon (*O. tschawytscha*) has been recorded weighing over 40 kg, although the average is about 9 kg. Chinook have black mouths and gums and become progressively darker until they die after spawning. Chinook are cultured for replacement in rivers affected by hydro-electric schemes on the American and Canadian coasts, but are not extensively farmed for the table. The chinook often swims as much as 1500-2000 miles up the Yukon or Frazer rivers to spawn, and this migratory feat, while producing eggs and milt and without feeding, is a major functional reason for its large size on entering the river.

The coho salmon (*O. kisutch*) is probably the best Pacific salmon for the table with its very red flesh and good smoking and freezing qualities. It is farmed in Russia, America and Japan. A silvery fish in saltwater the coho turns red when moving into freshwater to spawn. As well as the very prominent kype in the male, both sexes develop white nostrils.

The sockeye salmon (*O. nerka*), the most popular of the Pacific salmon for canning purposes, is known as the 'blue-back' when at sea because of its bright greenish-blue hue, but on entering freshwater it turns very bright red, with a greenish head.

The pink (*O. gorbuscha*) and chum salmon (*O. keta*) differ from the other Pacific salmon in that their young migrate to sea immediately after hatching instead of having a freshwater feeding period. The chum is a biggish (5 kg) slender fish which is very silver at sea, but develops red irregular blotches when coming into fresh water. The pink is much smaller, and is the species also found in the Atlantic as a result of the Russian releases.

All Pacific salmon species are at present being investigated for their food farming potential, and the farming of coho has already developed into an industry.

Oncorhynchus masou is a species mainly found in Northern Japan which is similar to *O. nerka*.

There are land-locked varieties of both Atlantic and Pacific salmon, the Atlantic land-locked races being mainly found in Eastern America and Northern Europe, and the Pacific ones, notably the kokanee variety of the sockeye, in the western USA and Canada.

3 Genus *Thymallus* The Grayling

The Grayling (*T. thymallus*) which is found in British freshwaters, spawns in summer like the coarse fish. It is the nearest member of the *Salmonini* to the other branch of the *Salmonidae*, the *Coregonini*, which includes certain whitefish. Although grayling have been cultured, they are usually considered deleterious to a trout or salmon fishery.

4 Genus *Salvelinus*

The members of genus *Salvelinus* are known as the chars; (in America many of the species referred to as trout are in fact chars).

The characteristic distinguishing feature of the chars is the vomer bone which is the longitudinal bone in the top of the mouth. In the trout and salmon it is flat and covered with teeth all the way down, whereas in the chars it is keel-shaped, and has very few teeth and only at the top. The chars are usually redder in colour than salmon and their spots are usually lighter in colour than the background.

Chars are not usually cultured for the table, but the American varieties such as the brook trout, the Dolly Varden trout and lake trout are cultured in the USA and Canada and in some European countries for restocking. Normally an inhabitant of colder waters, the European char is only found in deep lakes usually at high altitudes.

The chars feed at lower temperatures than rainbow trout or brown trout, and in very cold climates may therefore be better capable of weight-gain than even the rainbow trout, which grows very rapidly at higher temperatures.

Table 1 Differentiation between *S. salar* and *S. trutta*

Feature	Juvenile Fish	
	S. salar	*S. trutta*
Parr marks	10-12	9-10
Dorsal fin rays	10-12	8-10
Adipose fin	Black	Red tip
Ventral fins	Large and white	Smaller, orange red
Tail	Deep fork	Shallow fork
Upper lip	Short, only to mid-eye	Long, to behind eye
Scales between lateral line and adipose fin	13-16	11

Table 1 cont.

Adult Fish

Feature	S. salar	S. trutta
Scales between lateral line and adipose fin	13-16	11
Wrist (tail peduncle)	Very slim (grilse) Slim (Spring fish)	Stout and short
Tail	Swallow tail (grilse) Forked (Spring fish)	Flat-ended
Scale reading	Wide winter rings; usually no spawning marks	Narrow winter rings; usually many spawning marks on a large specimen

Table 2 The Salmonidae

Coregonus	*Coregonus lavaretus* (Powan)
Thymallus	*Thymallus thymallus* (Grayling)
Salvelinus	*Salvelinus fontinalis* (Brook trout) *Salvelinus malma* (Dolly Varden) *Salvelinus namaycush* (Lake trout) *Salvelinus alpinus* (European char)
Salmo	*Salmo trutta* (Brown/Sea trout) *Salmo salar* (Atlantic salmon) *Salmo gairdneri* (Rainbow trout/ Steelhead) *Salmo clarkii* (Cut-throat trout)
Oncorhynchus	*Oncorhynchus masou* (Japanese salmon) *Oncorhynchus kisutch* (Coho) *Oncorhynchus tschawytscha* (Chinook) *Oncorhynchus keta* (Chum) *Oncorhynchus nerka* (Sockeye) *Oncorhynchus gorbuscha* (Pink)

Chapter II
The Anatomy of Salmonid Fish

Salmonid fish are well adapted to their life style, being fast and sharp-eyed to catch their prey. Since they eat live food they have the typical short digestive tract of the carnivore. Many of the diseases of salmonid fish, or their signs, are directly related to the anatomy of the fish. The following descriptive chapter is therefore essential to allow the reader to understand the significance of the sites of disease in salmonids.

The anatomy of a typical salmonid is depicted in Fig 1. The description is given under the organ systems, as follows

   1 The integumentary system — skin and appendages.
   2 Muscular system — muscles and bones.
   3 Respiratory system — gills.
   4 Circulatory system — heart and blood vessels.
   5 Digestive system — mouth, stomach, intestine and associated glands.
   6 Excretory system — kidney and bladder.
   7 Reproductive system — ovaries and testes.
   8 Nervous system — brain, spinal cord and nerves.
   9 Endocrine system — pituitary, adrenal, and other hormone-producing glands.

1 The integumentary system

The skin of the salmonid is essential for waterproofing the fish as well as providing the armour plating of the scales. This function of keeping the water out, and fish tissue-fluids in, is performed by the epidermis. This is a very delicate clear covering which is draped over the scales, and possesses little glands, the goblet cells. These help to secrete the slimy mucus, a protective coating of infection-resistant slippery fluid, which also makes the fish difficult to hold. Sometimes

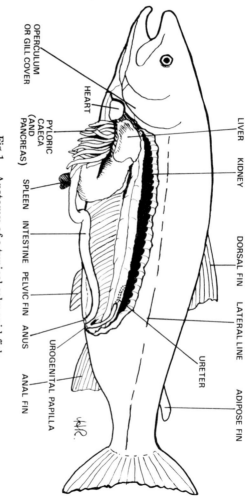

Fig 1   Anatomy of a typical salmonid fish.

OPERCULUM
OR GILL COVER

HEART

PYLORIC
CAECA
(AND
PANCREAS)

SPLEEN

INTESTINE

PELVIC FIN

ANUS

UROGENITAL PAPILLA

ANAL FIN

LIVER

KIDNEY

DORSAL FIN

LATERAL LINE

URETER

ADIPOSE FIN

skin parasite infections cause the epidermis to secrete a thicker, more viscid mucus, which gives it a bluish tinge, but usually it is clear.

Beneath the epidermis lie the scales — ovoid plates of bony material which are formed in small pockets, or scale beds. Scales develop on salmonids at the fry stage, and once a fish has its full quota of scales, it does not develop more as it increases in size. Consequently the scales must grow in step with the fish. Scales grow by accumulation of material round their edges, laid down in the form of concentric rings. When a fish is growing rapidly these rings are spaced far apart so that in the summer (or in the sea) the distance between rings is much greater than in winter. At spawning time, the salmonids do not feed, and in order to obtain sufficient calcium for their eggs or sperm they withdraw calcium from the outermost scale rings. This results in permanent scarring of the scale at that place (Fig 2). By examination of scales, salmon biologists are able to assess the age, number of spawnings, and even the fish's length at the end of each year of life. Occasionally a scale may be damaged, and a new scale grows in the scale pocket. This scale cannot recapitulate the previous life history of the fish and that area of the new scale is therefore blank.

Over the scales are the pigment cells — melanophores or black cells, irridiphores or silver cells, and xanthophores, which produce the yellow and red spots. The black and silver cells are under both nervous and hormonal (ie chemical) control. When fish are on a dark background they emphasize their black pigment cells, and on a light background, the silver cells. When they are depressed due to disease, fish frequently become darker in colour.

The strength of the skin is in the dermis — the layer below the scales. This is a very fibrous layer with considerable tensile strength.

2 The muscular system

The main swimming muscles of salmonids are arranged in a series of blocks or myotomes. This gives them considerable driving force on the tail. The myotomes are attached to the spine, the central bone, which is very flexible.

The fins are moved by small independent muscles. In addition to the usual fins, the salmonid fish are all characterized by a small appendage on the back, just in front of the

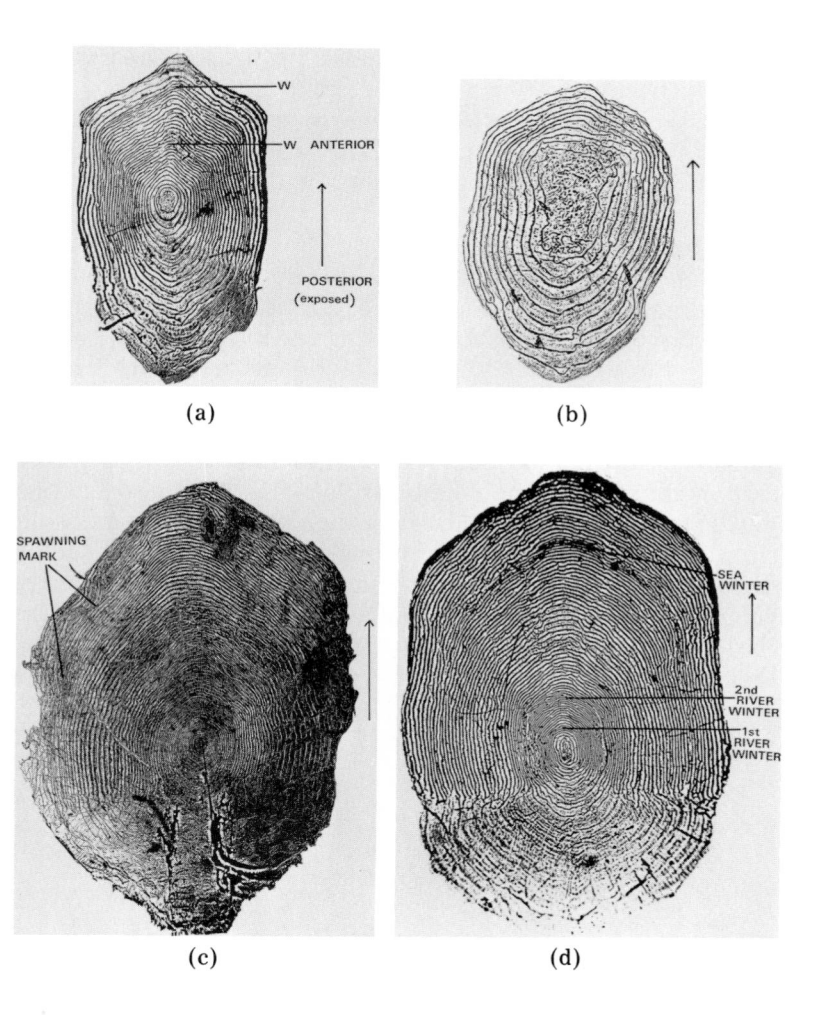

(a)   (b)

(c)   (d)

Fig 2   Scales from Atlantic salmon at different stages, showing features of the life cycle which may be determined by scale reading. (a) Scale from a two year old smolt showing two winter growth periods (W) separated by a summer band, with a second summer band with wide rings being laid down on the margin. The posterior part of the scale is rougher and more worn than the anterior, which is protected within the scale pocket. (b) A replacement scale formed after loss of the original scale. The central empty zone is scar tissue surrounded by 'normal' circuli. (c) Adult salmon scale showing a spawning mark, where calcium has been resorbed from the scale. (d) Grilse scale showing two years of river life (*cf* scale 2a) and one year in the sea. This is the normal pattern for most grilse in British rivers.

Photographs by courtesy of Dr L M Laird.

tail, which is known as the adipose fin because of its fatty internal structure.

The skeleton of the young fish, as with other animals, is formed of cartilage, which becomes calcified later and can have an important influence on certain diseases.

3 The respiratory system

Fish breathe by means of gills, a system of four sets of very fine tubes on either side of the throat through which the blood flows, and over which water is continually passed. In passing through the gills, the blood gives up its carbon dioxide to the water, and obtains oxygen from the water, through the gill wall. The respiratory surfaces of the gills, the lamellae, have to be very delicate so that the oxygen and carbon dioxide can be readily exchanged. They also contain mucus-producing cells and cells which excrete any excess salt from the blood as it passes through them. Obviously such a delicate structure on the outside of the body is highly vulnerable to injury via the water. The gills are protected on the outside by a bony shield called the operculum, and on the inside of the throat they have a set of comb-like

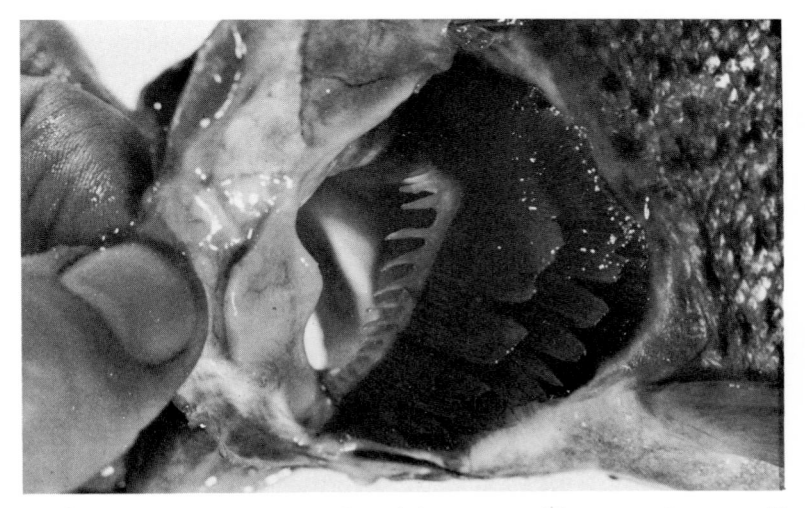

Fig 3   Respiratory system of a rainbow trout. The operculum, or gill cover is raised in this illustration to show the gills on their cartilaginous arches. The white teeth on the inner gill arch are the gill rakers. Water is continually passing over the gills, bringing essential oxygen, but they are favoured sites for parasites as they provide shelter and a rich food supply.

structures called gill rakers, which help to guide the food down to the gullet rather than over the gills (Fig 3).

4 The circulatory system

The circulatory system is the blood-transport system of the fish. The pump in the system is the heart, a muscular organ occupying the area at the base of the throat. It is a two-chambered pump (lacking the auxiliary pump for taking blood to the lungs, which is a feature of man and the higher animals). The blood passes from the triangular, very muscular ventricle, which provides the main pressure, in to the white, elastic-walled conus arteriosus. (Fig 4). This is an elastic pressure-balance converting the pumping of the heart into a steady surge of blood to the gills, from whence it passes to the rest of the body to deliver up oxygen to the tissues. Once it has passed through the gills its pressure is much reduced and its passage through the tissues is relatively slow. In the fine circulatory network of the tissues, the capillaries, the oxygen of the blood is replaced by carbon dioxide and waste

Fig 4   Heart of an Atlantic salmon. The heart is the main pump of the body and in this picture the large conical ventricle, with its coronary vessels is readily seen. The white structure is the conus arteriosus and the dark area the atrium or auricle.

products. The blood then returns via the vena cava or great vein, passing through the kidney on its way back to the heart. As the blood passes through the capillaries, some fluid, known as lymph, is lost to the tissues. This is the watery fluid which runs from a fresh fillet of fish. The lymph is returned to the circulation by a separate set of vessels, the lymphatics, which return it to the blood stream just before the heart.

5 The digestive system
This system is a relatively simple tube in the salmonids (Fig 5). It starts at the mouth, where the teeth are designed for capture not chewing. When ingested the food is quickly passed down the gullet or oesophagus to the stomach, a U shaped organ which can expand greatly to take large meals. It is in the stomach that the food is really chewed,, *ie* it is broken down by the action of acid and digestive enzymes as well as the crushing contractions of the muscles in the wall of the stomach. At the posterior end of the stomach where it joins the small intestine, there is a group of blind-ending sacs, the pyloric caeca. These usually number 30 to 80, and they lie conspicuously across the stomach when the fish is opened. They are covered with a considerable amount of white fatty tissue unless the fish has been starved. From the stomach, food passes through a one-way valve, the pylorus, to the

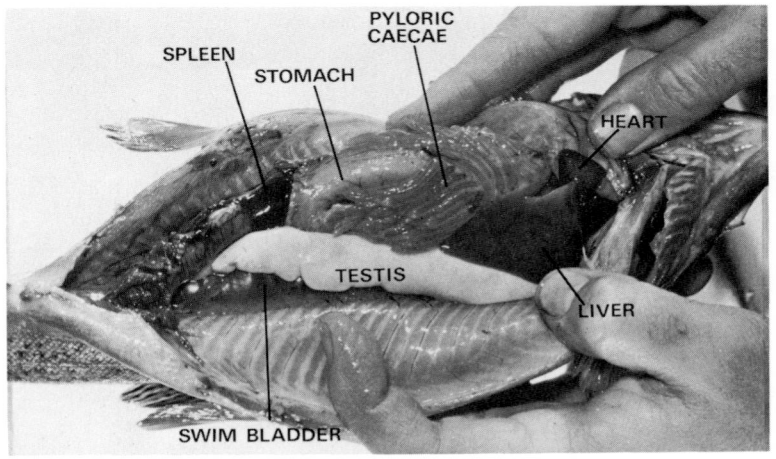

Fig 5   Ventral view of the abdomen of a rainbow trout at post-mortem. The abdominal cavity should be full, but without excessive fluid in it. The liver should not be pale or bronzed and there should be a small amount of fat around the pyloric caeca.

intestine, where the disintegrated food is acted upon by further enzymes. These break down the food to its constituent sugars, fats, and amino-acids (from proteins), which then pass into the blood stream of the intestinal wall for transport to the liver. The remaining food — roughage, snail shells, etc, travels on to the large intestine and is voided as faeces.

Associated with the digestive tract are two very important glands. One, the liver, is a large organ situated just in front of the stomach. It is a pinky-brown colour, soft, and easily ruptured. The liver is the main factory of the body, to which food molecules are taken in the blood from the intestine, for manufacture into the proteins, carbohydrates and fats of the fish's body. Inserted in the top of the liver is a small greenish sac — the gall bladder. When incised, this usually releases a greenish fluid called bile, which under normal conditions passes to the intestine through the bile duct, and aids with food breakdown.

Because of its importance in food metabolism, disease of the liver is very significant. The commonest liver abnormalities are excessive infiltration by unsuitable dietary fats and parasitism. Parasites are also frequently found in the gall bladder.

The other important associated digestive gland is the pancreas. This is a very diffuse structure which cannot be seen with the naked eye as it is scattered in bits and pieces throughout the fat surrounding the pyloric caecae. The pancreas has two functions, the production of pancreatic enzymes, which pass via the pancreatic duct to the intestine, and the production of insulin, which controls sugar metabolism and prevents fish from becoming diabetic. The pancreas is very significant in virus diseases, because it is a favourite site of multiplication for two of the most important salmonid viruses.

Many species of fish possess a swim bladder, which is a hydrostatic organ used to trim buoyancy at the appropriate depth (Fig 6). The swim bladder may also have a function as a hollow organ for receiving deep, low frequency sounds. In the salmonids it has a connection with the back of the throat so that the fish can quickly squeeze out air and drop to the bottom. Any blockage of this duct, or damage to the swim bladder wall, can result in considerable swimming problems for the fish.

29

Fig 6   Swim bladder. This illustration shows the abdominal cavity with the majority of the viscera removed. The swim bladder may be dilated but should not contain excess fluid or be thickened and it should not be tightly filled with gas. The kidney is immediately below the swim bladder in this picture.

6 The excretory system

The kidney is the main filter of the body. It filters blood through a sieve-like apparatus called the glomerulus and passes it through tubes to paired ducts, the ureters, which carry it to the bladder. In salmonids this is a small thin-walled structure above the anus. The duct from the bladder drains via the urogenital opening, which is also the exit for eggs.

The kidney of the salmonids is a long black structure in the top of the abdomen, extending from the back of the head to the vent. The vena cava runs through the centre of the kidney and on its outer surface may be seen the narrow white ureters, wending towards the bladder.

In higher animals the kidney is purely a selective filter, but in the fishes it also contains the haemopoietic tissue, especially at the front end of the kidney. This is the tissue which makes the oxygen-carrying red blood cells, and defensive white blood cells, and also stores them until they are needed. The other site where this takes place is the spleen, a large black organ attached to the wall of the intestine. This haemopoietic tissue of kidney and spleen is very important in disease as it is affected by a number of serious bacterial and viral agents. It also contains a network of traps, the fixed macrophage cells, which catch any microbes passing through in the blood stream and usually succeed in destroying them.

7 The reproductive system

The gonads of the salmonids comprise paired ovaries in the female and testes in the male. In the immature or resting state they lie in the anterior of the abdomen, above and on either side of the stomach. At sexual maturity, under the control of the hormones from the pituitary gland, they develop to extend the full length of the abdomen.

The ovary consists of germinal cells, some of which grow to the size of a pea to form the orange-coloured ova or eggs. Others stay small as the cells for subsequent spawnings.

At spawning the skin of both male and female becomes thicker and more shiny, and also the urogenital opening swells up. Eggs are released into the abdomen as the supporting capsule ruptures, and are pushed on a tide of fluid to the urogenital opening by contractions of the female's abdominal muscles and by small sweeping hair-like cilia inserted in certain parts of the lower abdominal wall.

Semen, known as 'milt' in fish, is excreted from the testes by bodily contraction and passes into the water as a cloud of living, wriggling sperm cells. In the wild this occurs in the redd prepared by the female, but hatcherymen assist the process artificially.

8 The nervous system

The nervous system of salmonid fish reflects their behaviour. Salmon home on their sense of smell, hunt with their eyes, and are creatures almost entirely of reflex. Consequently they have a well developed olfactory area at the front of the brain, which connects directly with the nostrils. These are paired sacs on the snout and have a continual flow of water over their sensitive tissue. The area of the brain responsible for sight (the optic lobes) comprises two large rounded structures occupying almost a third of the brain's volume, whereas the cerebral tissue (corresponding to the massive cerebral hemispheres, or thinking area, of the human brain) comprises two very small areas on the side of the brain stem (Fig 7). The brain is extended backwards, as the spinal cord, from which arise nerves to muscles, organs and skin. The

31

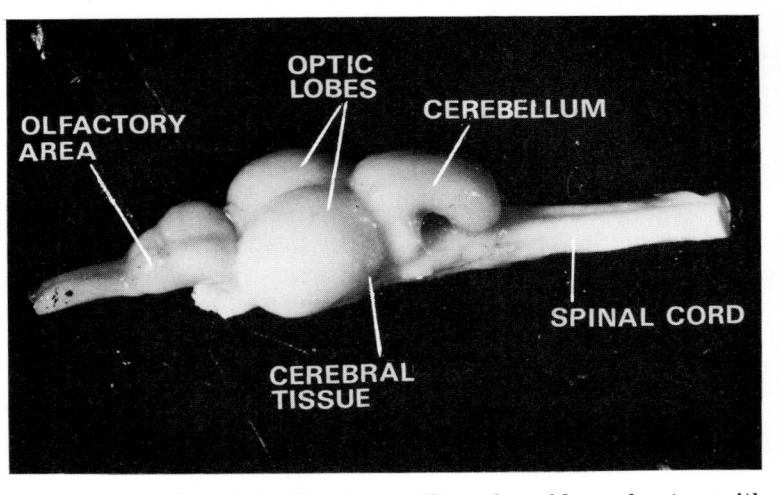

Fig 7   Brain of an Atlantic salmon. The salmonids are hunters with keen eyesight and a good sense of smell. Hence the front part of the brain, which is concerned with smell and is continuous with the nostril, is quite well developed, and the paired optic lobes of the brain (the large domes) comprise its largest component. The thinking part, or cerebral cortex, is very small and confined to just below and behind the optic lobes. The cerebellum is responsible for the continuous co-ordination of information received via the spinal cord from various parts of the body, regarding position and activity.

spinal cord passes down the middle of the vertebrae of the spinal column, which gives it considerable protection. The skin contains certain nerve endings which can detect touch and pain. The most interesting of the surface sensory structures are the lateral lines — symmetrical, long, narrow, fluid-filled tubes extending from the back of the head to the tail, with pores opening to the exterior, and sensitive nerve endings lining their inside wall. The lateral line is believed to receive pressure waves in the water.

The eye of the salmon, as with all fish, has no eyelids, but internally is similar to that of other animals. The lens is round and completely clear in the normal fish, but in certain disease conditions becomes cloudy. The eye is also one of the sites with extremely delicate blood vessels and is therefore very vulnerable to rupture of capillaries, *eg* by gas bubbles in certain circumstances.

The ears of salmonid fish do not have an outlet and although they may detect some vibrations, their main function is balance. They are located within the skull, just behind the eyes, and when they are damaged by disease the fish is unable to balance properly.

9 Endocrine system

The endocrine glands are small groups of cells which have a significance for the body way beyond their size. They secrete chemicals into the blood stream, hormones, which act on distant sites such as the gonads, skin or blood vessels. The most important endocrine gland, the pituitary, which has been called the 'conductor of the endocrine orchestra', is located in a very secure site below the brain.

The adrenal is a gland producing several important hormones including the fear hormone, adrenaline. It is located within the haemopoietic tissue at the anterior end of the kidney. The thyroid gland, producing growth hormone, is elusive in the salmonids, often scattered randomly around the tissues of the throat area. Salmonids and other fish also have two endocrine structures with as yet unknown functions. The Corpuscles of Stannius are small white spots, placed laterally in the mid-kidney tissue and usually three or four can be seen on the surface of the kidney. The pseudobranch is a red, vestigial gill-like structure on the inside face of each operculum.

Chapter III
Husbandry of Salmonid Fish

Successful farming of salmon and trout relies upon a high standard of husbandry and stockmanship. This in turn depends on sound application of the principles of fish biology, agriculture and allied sciences, within the context of economics.

A BIOLOGICAL REQUIREMENTS
A knowledge of the environmental requirements is essential in order to obtain good growth and health in salmonid farming, as in other types of intensive livestock production.

1 Oxygen
Where possible the incoming supply of water should be fully saturated with oxygen. The ability of water to take oxygen into solution is governed by temperature, pressure, and its dissolved salts. The higher the temperature, the less oxygen is contained in fully saturated water, *eg* in fresh water with 1 atmosphere of pressure at 5°C, oxygen solubility = 12.8 ppm; at 20°C, oxygen solubility = 9.2 ppm. As the salinity is increased this solubility is reduced, and the oxygen solubilities in full sea-water at the same temperatures and pressure are 10.0 ppm and 6.7 ppm respectively. If atmospheric pressure is reduced, the solubility is also reduced and this may be significant for fish farms at very high altitudes.

The minimum level of dissolved oxygen for trout and salmon is about 5.5 ppm, or about 7 ppm for eggs. In fish farms, as the temperature rises, the fish are usually fed more heavily and their rate of oxygen consumption is markedly increased. At the same time faeces, and perhaps unused feed, build up on the bottom and decompose, taking up oxygen in the process. During the hours of darkness, any aquatic plants

34

present, *eg* algae, will also be using up oxygen. So, even if the incoming water is fully saturated, under conditions of heavy stocking rates and high temperatures, the amount of dissolved oxygen present may drop to dangerously low levels. It is therefore advisable to use splashboards at the inlet of each pond to assist saturation, and to possess aerators for use in danger periods (high temperatures, medication, etc). Rates of flow and depth of water must be adjusted so that the consequent water exchange rate is adequate for the density of fish stocked, water temperature and feeding rate. Care should be taken to ensure that calculations of the usable volume of the pond exclude areas of stagnant water. Finally it should be borne in mind that fish consume oxygen at a higher rate when they are small, *ie* 1 kg of fry need more water than 1 kg of growers.

2 Temperature
Salmonids will generally survive underneath thin ice cover and at temperatures up to around 25°C. However, above about 20°C, oxygen levels become limiting as the dissolved oxygen concentration of water falls with rising temperature and it is necessary to starve the fish in order to minimize oxygen requirements. Incubation of eggs is best carried out at temperatures below 13°C.

3 pH
The pH value of the water is a measure of its acidity or alkalinity and is measured on a scale whose range is from 0 (very acid) to 14 (very alkaline) with the neutral point at 7. Since it is a logarithmic scale a change of 0.1 pH units represents a marked change in acidity. It is important that the pH should not fluctuate but remain stable at some point within the approximate range 6.4-8.4, and pH may easily be measured by portable meters. Variations in pH stress the fish and are less likely to occur if the water is 'buffered' as in limestone areas. This is because such water contains large amounts of dissolved salts especially calcium salts, which resist changes in pH and which favour natural plant and animal life. Acidic water is found in regions deficient in calcium and associated with igneous rock. Very acidic waters may arise due to mineral acids leached out of the soil by spates. The consequent low pH can cause bleeding (haemorrhages) on the gills and heavy mortalities. It is

possible in such circumstances to add lime (calcium carbonate) to the inflow water in order to increase resistance to changes in pH.

4 Ammonia

Ammoniacal substances are produced as excretory products by salmon and trout and are usually in a mixture of two forms: free ammonia (NH_3) and ionized ammonia (NH_4^+). The free ammonia is by far the more toxic of the two substances and concentrations as low as 0.017 ppm NH_3 are harmful to trout, causing damage to the gills and reduced growth. The relative proportions of free ammonia and ionized ammonia are dependent primarily upon the pH of the water, and the higher the pH, the greater the proportion of free ammonia, *ie* the toxic form. Therefore, although alkaline water has the great advantage that it is usually stable in pH, it has the disadvantage that any build-up in wastes is likely to be more dangerous than in acidic water.

5 Toxic substances

It is by now obvious that fish continually excrete substances which are potentially harmful to themselves. Accumulation of faeces encourages the build-up of ammonia and also increases the amount of suspended matter in the water. Suspended solids can harm fish in two ways: by mechanical irritation and clogging of the gills, and by removing oxygen from the water during decomposition. This may be a problem when organic matter enters the water supply following a storm. In a fish farm it is very important to maintain an adequate water exchange rate and to clean the ponds regularly in order to prevent accumulation of waste material (this is generally not practical with earthen ponds where a degree of self-cleaning may exist due to bacterial action of the mud bottom).

A particular water supply may therefore have insufficient oxygen for fish health due to its removal from solution, and this is frequently the cause of heavy mortalities when certain toxic substances, *eg* silage liquor, enter a water supply. However, water drawn from a spring, borehole, or well may have insufficient oxygen due to lack of surface oxygenation from the air. Such water may also have a supersaturation of other gases (notably nitrogen) and this can cause disease in fish even if the oxygen levels are adequate. Occasionally ground water may also contain gases such as hydrogen sulphide which are toxic to fish. These problems can usually be adequately controlled by artificial aeration of the water supply before it enters the farm. By this means excess nitrogen and other gases may be blown off and the water saturated with oxygen. Use of a meter for dissolved oxygen will assist evaluation of the supply.

Heavy metal ions may occur in water due to factors such as metal ores in the rock strata, the composition of pipes, or the presence of industrial effluent. These comprise ions such as iron, lead and copper which, except at very low levels, are toxic to fish. Iron salts can be a particular problem and may coat the surface of both eggs and gills causing asphyxiation and heavy losses. In addition many substances are extremely toxic to fish and may enter the water supply accidentally, *eg* sheep dips and weedkillers, and even maliciously in the case of cyanide. The chlorine contained in much potable water is toxic to fish and most of the chemicals used for treating fish diseases have some toxic effects. Often they also remove some oxygen from the water which imposes additional stress.

6 Salinity

It is possible to farm rainbow trout entirely in fresh water, although salmon require both freshwater and marine facilities. However, rearing rainbow trout in salt water causes an increase in growth rate. For rapid growth, intermediate salinities may be preferable for rainbow trout, in contrast to smoltified Atlantic salmon which will not usually tolerate salinities lower than 30 parts per thousand. Transferring rainbow trout from fresh water straight into full strength (34 parts per thousand salinity) sea-water cannot be undertaken before they are about 100 g each. Acclimatization of salmonids to high salinities may usually be accomplished earlier by gradual introduction to increasing concentrations of seawater.

The advantages of marine farming of rainbow trout may be summarized as follows:

(i) probable increase in growth rate due to salinity
(ii) very stable physical and chemical environment with high buffering capacity due to dissolved salts.
(iii) less temperature variation than fresh water (excluding ground water), with winter temperatures which are often relatively higher.

Although abundant sea-water may therefore be preferable to (often limited) fresh water, it should be remembered that sea-water contains significantly less dissolved oxygen when stocking densities are being calculated.

7 Food and nutrition

Salmon and trout are carnivorous fish in their natural environment, so it is hardly surprising that they require high protein diets under farmed conditions. The earliest salmonid culturists used liver or abattoir scraps, and even now the Danish trout industry is heavily dependent on industrial fish supplies as its basic food source. However, there are many advantages in using commercially prepared pelleted foods. For salmonids these diets must contain a high proportion of fish meal which is very expensive. They also contain some carbohydrate, which supplies energy, and essential vitamins, fatty acids and minerals.

Economical production should aim at fast growth rates with minimal waste and the method of feeding is therefore very important. The Food Conversion Rate is expressed as

$$\text{FCR} = \frac{\text{weight of food consumed}}{\text{increase of weight of fish}}$$

Fish convert food into growth progressively less efficiently as they increase in size. Trout reared to 200 g on high protein pellets might have an overall FCR of 1.4, *ie* 1.4 kg of pellets required to produce 1 kg of trout. If their FCR was calculated as fry, it might be only 0.8 because pellets usually contain very much less moisture than trout fry (the farmer is not really getting something for nothing). Conversely a trout farmer feeding minced seafish with a high moisture content would probably be satisfied with a FCR of 5.0 for trout reared to 200 g, or 4.5 if he added some form of binder. When calculating FCR's the weights of any mortalities should also be recorded and stated, or included in the sum. It is only by careful attention to FCR that a farmer can evaluate whether he is feeding correctly.

Incorrect feeding rates are likely to cause poor conversion rates due to both physical wastage and consequent nutritional and disease problems. For example, too little food will cause losses from starvation, cannibalism and parasitism. Too much food will tend to foul the water with unused feed, removing oxygen and predisposing to various infectious diseases. Poor conversion efficiency is a common symptom of disease problems in fish, particularly where the disease is a slow insidious process of reduced growth, rather than a sudden 'acute' flare-up with heavy mortalities. Such 'chronic' disease states may pass unremarked if the poor conversion efficiency, ie high FCR, is not observed and investigated.

Feeding rates are usually computed from charts and are based upon water temperature and fish weight. Feed may be given to the stock by hand or by automatic feeders operated either by time switchgear or by the fish themselves. Hand feeding allows the farmer to observe the behaviour of the stock. Self-feeders ('demand' feeders) allow the fish to regulate their own needs. They seem unable to avoid over-feeding when the temperature is high although it is probable that maximum food conversion efficiency is attained at a daily intake considerably less than that required to satisfy fish (ie ad-lib feeding). A problem with self-feeders is that more frequent grading may be necessary, as they seem to result in increased variation in size among a population; this may be due to a 'pecking order' becoming established around the feeder. Giving the ration equally throughout the day rather than all at once is facilitated by automatic feeders, and may assist conversion efficiency, especially with fry, which should be fed up to eight times per day. It also helps to spread out daily oxygen requirements, and therefore is more economical on water.

B   CYCLE OF FARMING OPERATIONS

Spawning in the Northern hemisphere generally occurs from October to February, depending on the species. Under farming conditions, the male and female fish are manually stripped of their milt and ova which are mixed together. After fertilization has occurred, the eggs are placed in incubation systems. Development and hatching time are related to water temperature, and daily attention is necessary to ensure that dead eggs do not increase the spread of fungi by either the use of fungistats (notably malachite green) or removal of such eggs. Some farmers prefer to buy-in eggs from another source (eg the Southern hemisphere in order to obtain a summer hatch). In this case it is necessary to wait until they are 'eyed eggs' (ie the embryonic eye has become visible), after which the eggs become far more resistant to the trauma of handling and transport. It is also advisable to ensure that any bought-in eggs are bathed in a suitable disinfectant before introduction to the hatchery.

After hatching has occurred the young fish feed on the contents of their yolk sac for several weeks and are called yolk-sac fry or 'alevins'. The farmer must clean away the empty egg shells and ensure that water flows are adequate to supply oxygen and remove metabolic wastes. This latter task becomes increasingly critical once the fry have commenced to feed, at which stage they are usually transferred to some form of early-rearing facility. Young rainbow trout cannot generally be reared in earth ponds due to the danger of Whirling disease at this stage. However, in regions where this disease occurs, it can be avoided if the fry are kept in concrete or fibreglass tanks until they reach about 7 cm in length.

As the fish grow they require to be graded in order to prevent a large spread in unit weight among a particular stock, which would allow the larger fish to grow to the detriment of the smaller. Grading is normally performed once while within the fry tanks and then up to four times while the fish are within the on-growing facility. The method of grading depends on the size of the fish as well as the type of farm, and there is considerable scope for automation. Other important daily routines, such as cleaning inlet screens, filters and tanks, and repairing eroded banks and channels, are vital to prevent losses due to systems failures.

C   FISH FARMING SYSTEMS

There is a wide variety of technological systems available to aid the three stages of incubation, early-rearing, and on-growing. For incubation, traditional wooden hatchery trays are increasingly being replaced by vertically stacked incubators or vertical embryonators, which permit economies in space and water usage and ease operating problems. Early-rearing tanks are commonly rectangular or circular in design, and are fabricated in either concrete or fibreglass.

On-growing facilities comprise the major item of capital cost on trout farms and are often similar to the Danish systems of excavated earth ponds in parallel, feeding into a central outlet channel which also contains fish. These earth ponds are unlined and usually measure about 30 x 10 x 1½ m deep. Such earth pond systems are often used where the terrain is suitable, easily excavated and not too porous. Each pond requires about three exchanges of water per day in order to hold over a ton of fish at a stocking density of about 5 kg/m³. Recently there has been a trend towards more intensive systems such as raceways, which were pioneered in the USA and usually comprise parallel sets of narrow channels in series. There are often falls from one channel to the next in the series with splash-boards for aeration purposes. Raceways are usually constructed in materials such as concrete, which resists erosion and permits higher flow rates than earth ponds, and correspondingly higher water exchange rates and stocking densities (*eg* 3 exchanges/hour and 32 kg/m³ respectively). Where the terrain is unsuitable for construction of raceways, circular tanks may be used. These may be constructed with a peripheral inlet pipe and central drain, in order to provide a vortex and a consequent degree of self-cleaning. Unlike the cheaper earth ponds, raceways and circular tanks are quickly drained, cleaned, and disinfected; also the more intensive stocking and design of such systems permits better observation and eases operations such as grading and feeding, *ie* gives better control. Other systems, which are particularly used for marine culture of salmonids, include floating nets and netted enclosures. It is particularly difficult to achieve adequate control of such systems, but their capital cost is often minimal in relation to alternative facilities.

Fresh water is an increasingly scarce resource, and suitable supplies can be evaluated for fish farming in terms of both their minimum flow rate and temperature range. These factors determine the stocks which may be carried and the growth rates which may be achieved. For example in Scotland production of 1 ton *pa* of trout to a unit weight of about 200 g generally requires in the region of 4.5-7.5 l/sec (60-100 gpm) and an average production cycle of about 18 months can be assumed. Where water flows are inadequate, attempts may be made to recirculate using filter beds and pumps. However, the large quantities of water involved require extremely large and costly filters. Provision of pumping facilities will often permit construction of a farm where gravity-fed water is not available, *eg* beside a lake, although this introduces the risk of mechanical breakdown.

The choice of system must take into account the relative problems and advantages of each in terms of the natural topography of the site. However, the ultimate design of the

41

farm is likely to reflect how much money the farmer is prepared to pay to reduce the risks involved to what he considers an acceptable level. The possibility of major losses due to disease generally represents that risk which the fish farmer can most readily reduce by good management.

Chapter IV Infectious Diseases

Some of the major losses in salmonid culture are due to factors such as poisons, incorrect nutrition, or systems failures. However, most losses are caused by disease processes involving living agents. It is important to know that all animals and plants consist of greater or lesser aggregates of cells, which are small self-contained 'factories' making essential components such as bone, skin or nerve. With the single exception of viruses, the living agents which cause disease in fish are also cellular in nature.

In this chapter diseases caused by living agents are grouped together according to the aetiology, *ie* the nature of the infectious agent involved. This is because many diseases can be caused by closely related organisms and rational therapy of each group of diseases is dependent on a knowledge of the differences between their agents.

These diseases may be classified as:

    A Parasitic diseases
    B Bacterial diseases
    C Viral diseases
    D Fungal diseases
    E Diseases of complex or uncertain aetiology

A PARASITIC DISEASES

A parasite is an animal which spends part or all of its life living at the expense of another animal, known as the host. Parasites may be found in every tissue of the host and are particularly common on external surfaces. In the diseases which follow, the host is the salmonid fish but the parasites are of tremendous diversity. In the wild, salmonids have small numbers of parasites causing little if any injury, but in the farm or hatchery situation they can build up to considerable levels with harmful results. Parasites range in size from the microscopic to those which can be easily seen with the naked

Fig 8 Classification of salmonid parasites of economic significance

Protozoans

1 *Ceratomyxa*	6 *Hexamita* (= *Octomitus*)
2 *Costia* (= *Ichtyobodo*)	7 *Oodinium* and *Cryptocaryon*
3 *Henneguya*	8 *Plistophora*
4 *Ichthyophthirius*	9 *Scyphidia* 'complex'
5 *Myxosoma*	10 *Trichodina* 'complex'

Metazoans

Acanthocephalans

Cestodes
1 *Diphyllobothrium*
2 *Eubothrium*
3 *Triaenophorus*

Crustaceans
1 *Argulus*
2 *Lernaea*
3 *Lepeophtheirus*
4 *Salmincola*
5 'Others' (eg *Ergasilus, Achtheres*)

Nematodes
1 *Anisakis*
2 *Cystidicola*
3 Filariids
4 'Others'

Metazoans (cont)

Trematodes

Digenetic flukes
1 *Cotylurus*
2 *Cryptocotyle*
3 *Diplostomum*

Monogenetic flukes
1 *Dactylogyrus*
2 *Diplozoon*
3 *Discocotyle*
4 *Gyrodactylus*

Others
1 Lampreys
2 Leeches
3 Mussel Glochidia

eye. They are usually divided up into the *protozoa*, or single celled parasites, and the *metazoa*, or multicellular parasites (Fig 8).

Protozoans
Protozoa can only be seen properly with a microscope. Many can survive unfavourable conditions by having a spore stage in their life cycle, when their cell wall is very resistant to heat, disinfectants and drugs. They are very varied in size and shape and live mainly on the skin and gills of salmonid fish, although a few serious diseases are caused by *protozoa* which infect internal organs.

1 *Ceratomyxa*
Ceratomyxa are myxosporidian parasites like the causative agent of Whirling Disease. They can cause damage to almost any soft tissue where they are recognized by the characteristic shape of the spores.

2 *Costia* or *Ichtyobodo*
This is a very small pear-shaped protozoan (Fig 9) which propels itself by means of whip-like hairs called flagellae. It is found on gills and skin surfaces and is of major importance in fry. *Costia* is about the same size as fish skin cells, but these are non-motile, *ie* do not move about. Its small size means that it is readily overlooked and is best identified (high magnification) by its jerky spiral movements.

3 *Henneguya*
This group of parasites is found in the muscle and skin of wild salmon and sea trout, and is responsible for 'milky-flesh disease'. It is characterized by tadpole-shaped spores, with two eye-spots, or 'polar capsules' (Fig 10).

4 *Ichthyophthirius*
This is the causative agent of White Spot or 'Ich'. It is a natural parasite of carp and goldfish and its occurrence in salmonids can usually be traced back to contact with coarse fish. It grows within the skin of fish and has a complex life cycle involving multiplication both on the host and in the water (Fig 11a) (see frontispiece for illustration). The adult parasite, as it emerges from the fish, is a large (up to 1 mm) round, hairy, often brown-coloured parasite. It has a very

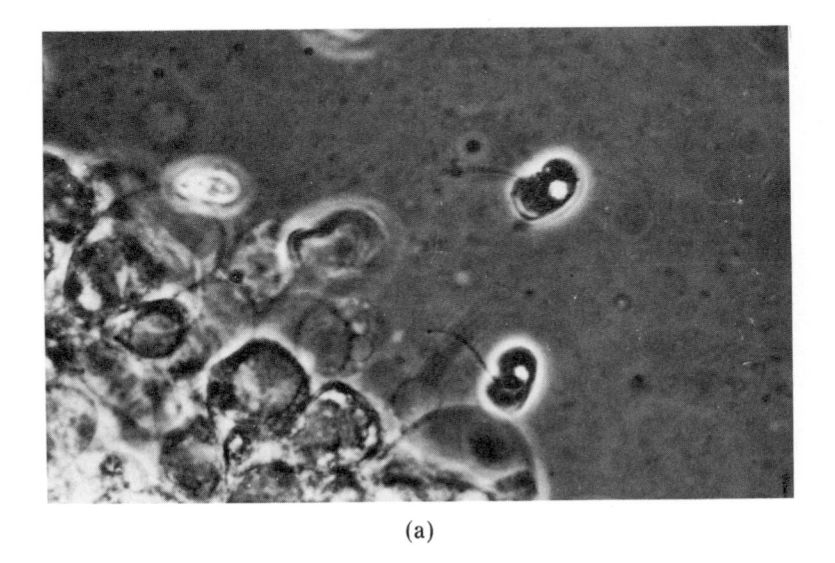

(a)

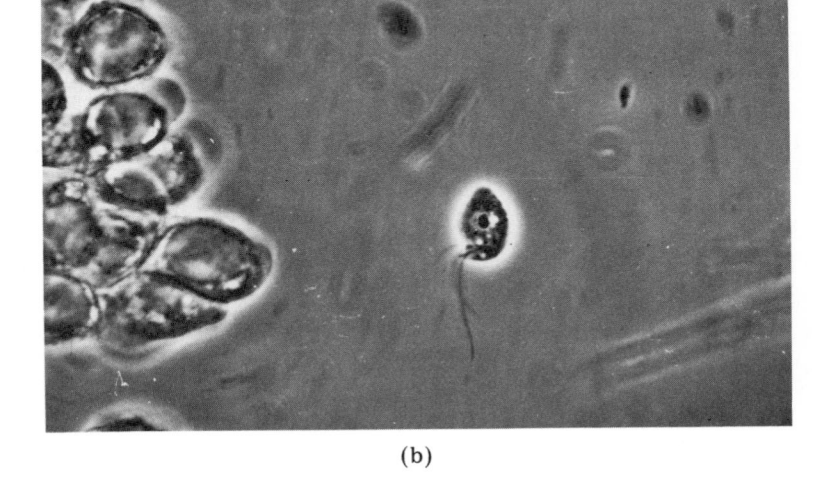

(b)

Fig 9 *Costia necatrix*. This parasite has a free swimming and an attached stage. It is very small, and the illustrations are magnified at least 1200 times so that the highest magnifications are needed when examining preparations under the microscope. (a) *Costia* swimming free. (b) Free swimming *Costia* becoming modified for attachment. (c) Two attached forms of *Costia* on the gill of an Atlantic salmon alevin.

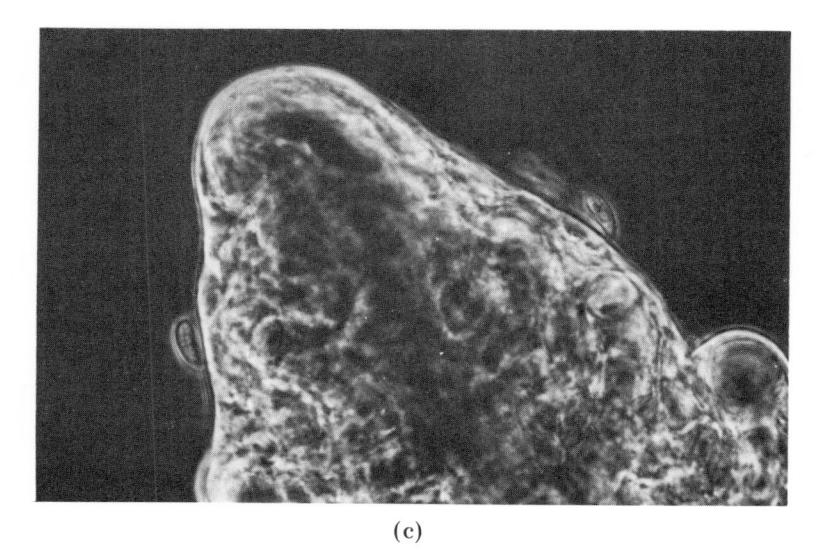

(c)

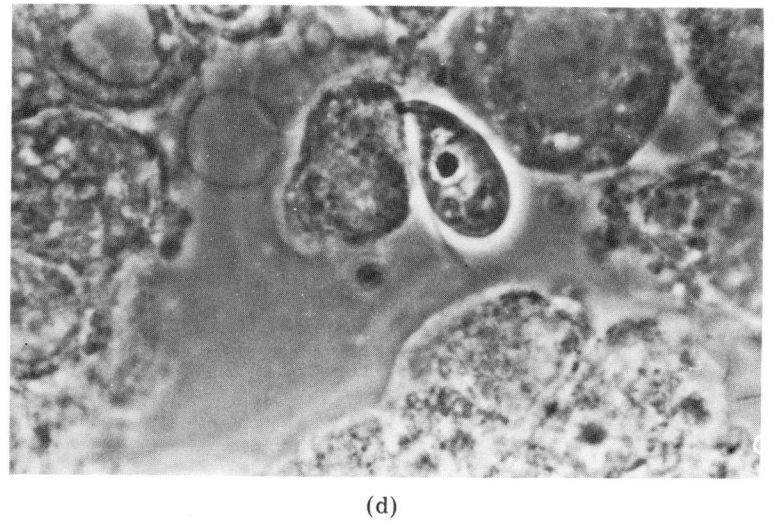

(d)

(d) *Costia* attached to an epidermal cell in a wet mount preparation from the skin of an Atlantic salmon. This specimen is enlarged 3000 times.

Photographs by courtesy of Mr C H Aldridge.
Copyright, Unilever Research Laboratories.

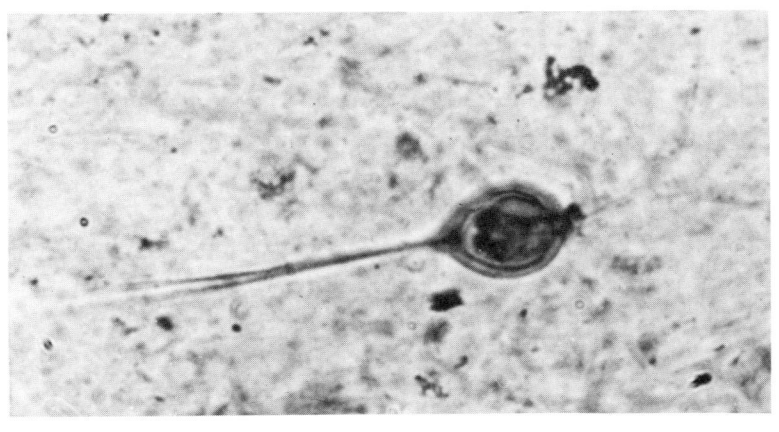

Fig 10 *Henneguya.* This sporozoan parasite is shown here in a smear from the muscles of a Coho salmon. The spores are encapsulated with two projections extending from the rear. This smear is magnified some 1200 times.

Photograph by courtesy of Mr D Bucke.

obvious, and characteristic horseshoe-shaped nucleus, and moves very slowly, if at all. It breaks out of the 'white spot' on the fish, encysts on the bottom of a pond, and out of the cyst pass some 500 small pear-shaped infectious stages, which invade any fish with which they can make contact. They penetrate the skin and turn into the next stage, which is a rapidly revolving, globular, light-coloured parasite (about 0.2 mm). This develops into the mature adult parasite to continue the cycle at a rate which is increased at higher temperatures. Examination of a skin-scraping, or of material squeezed from a 'white spot' frequently shows both of the host stages of the parasite (Fig 12).

5 *Myxosoma*

The parasite which causes Whirling disease is a small protozoan which has a life cycle involving a parasitic phase and a free-living phase. It must spend up to six months in

Fig 12 *Ichthyophthirius* (a) Smear of rainbow trout fry skin showing concentrically ringed scales (S) and the two stages of the 'Ich' parasite. The small rapidly revolving protozoan has just invaded the skin, but the larger form is mature and ready to leave the host. The scales which are just under 1 mm in diameter give some indication of the relative sizes. (b) Life cycle of *Ichthyophthirius multifiliis.*

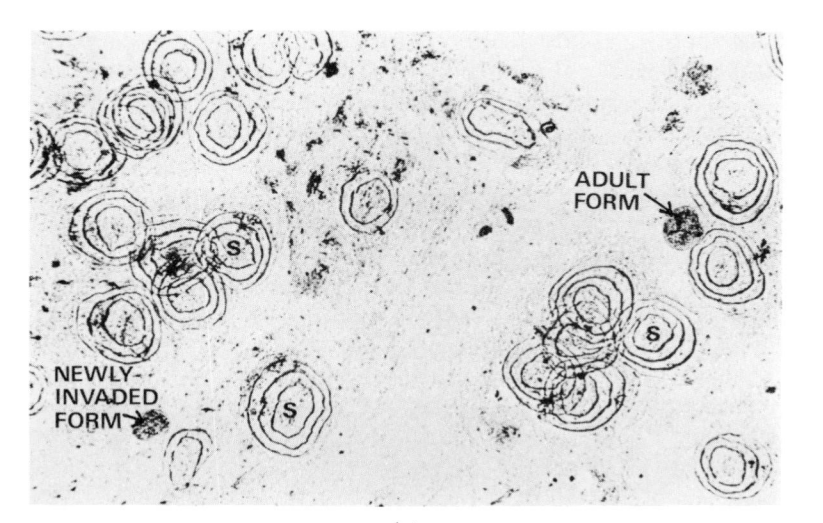

(a)

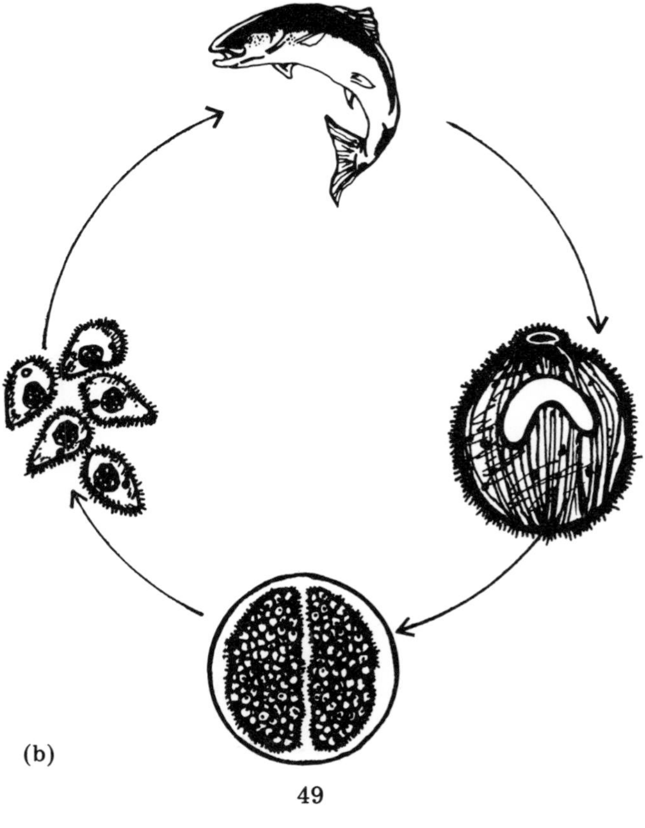

(b)

49

mud being 'conditioned' before being able to parasitize rainbow trout — the only species seriously affected. Once it has been ingested by a trout, the conditioned parasite leaves its protective cyst and invades the gut wall. From there it passes to the cartilage of the head. It can only parasitize young fish before their cartilages have hardened into bone, but once it penetrates the cartilages of the skull and spine it can, if present in any numbers, cause a severe reaction there.

Diagnosis is by chopping or scraping cartilage from the back of the head of suspect fish onto a slide and examining it for the characteristic parasitic spores (Fig 13).

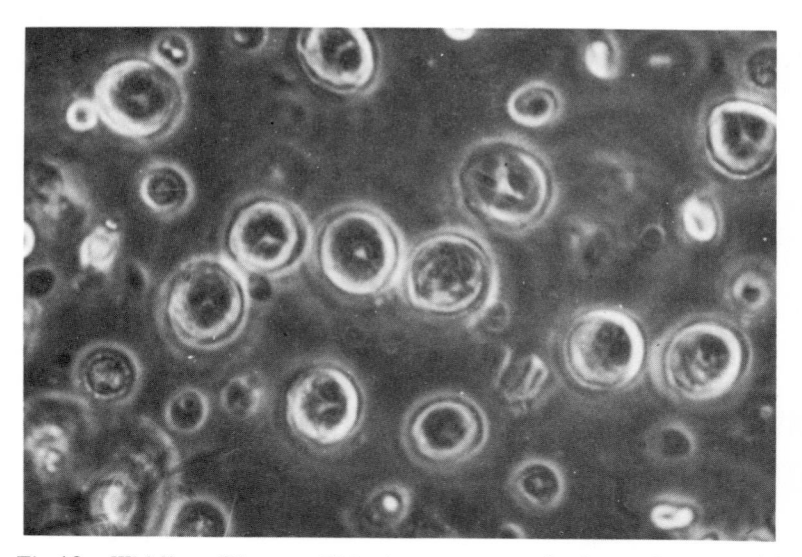

Fig 13   Whirling Disease. This is a smear of chopped-up cranial cartilages of a fish dying of whirling disease. The *Myxosoma* spores, characteristic of the disease, show a shiny edge with two eye spots, or polar capsules, and are best seen under the 40x objective.
Photograph by courtesy of Dr M Halliday.

6 *Hexamita* or *Octomitus*

This is a pear-shaped, very small, and very active parasite of the gall bladder and intestine, usually of rainbow trout (Fig 14). It moves rapidly by means of its long flagellae; in microscope preparations of smears of gut contents or gall bladder, it is usually the quick movement which attracts attention at low magnification. Its characteristic shape can be used for identification under the 40x lens.

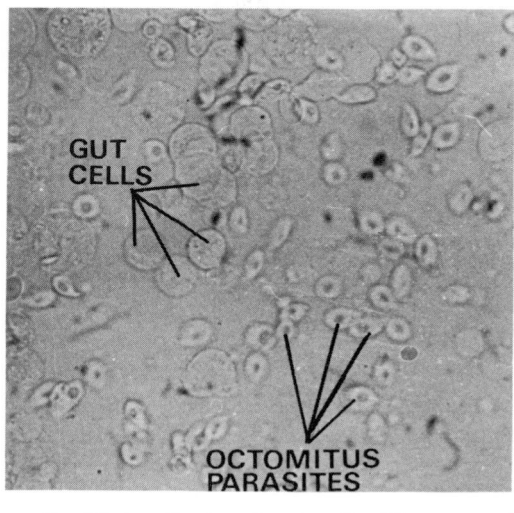

Fig 14   *Hexamita (Octomitus)* and gut cells. These parasites are very active and difficult to see (or photograph). They are pear-shaped and half the size of the gut cells, which are also visible in this smear of gut contents viewed under 40x magnification.

Photograph by courtesy of Dr T Håstein.

7 *Oodinium* and *Cryptocaryon*

These parasites have been observed in salmonids held at high density in marine aquaria, but have not yet emerged as major problems in the farm situation. *Oodinium* (Fig 15) is probably a dinoflagellate (p. 73) but, like the protozoan *Cryptocaryon*, lives on the skin of salmonids in salt water.

8 *Plistophora*

These are the smallest parasites affecting salmonids and may occur widely causing major losses, especially in North American trout farms. They have a complex life cycle, but the stage most readily recognized comprises a large number of spores which form a whitish cyst growing within the muscles or gills. These cysts may reach a considerable size, and the contents, when examined under 40x magnification, appear as minute, shiny spores, either oval or comma-shaped.

9 *Scyphidia* 'complex'

This complex includes the organisms *Scyphidia*, *Epistylis*, and *Glossatella*. All have the common feature that they merely use the skin of the fish as an attachment, or base, and

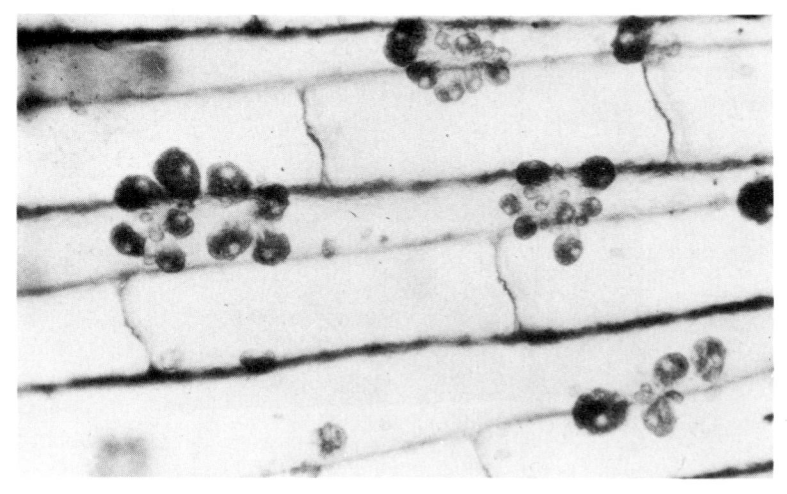

Fig 15 *Oodinium.* These parasites are best seen on the fins or gills when they can be observed growing out from sites on fin rays.
Photograph by courtesy of Dr R Bootsma.

feed off material passing them in the water (*cf* a barnacle living on a ship's hull). They are cylindrical or flask-shaped, and the stalk attaching them to the host may support several individuals. They are bigger than *Costia* or *Trichodina* (p. 45) and have a characteristic shape (Fig. 16). If they are of any significance, they will be present in large numbers in skin-scrapings.

10 *Trichodina* 'complex'
This complex includes the organisms *Trichodina, Trichodinella,* and *Chilodonella.* These parasites are larger than *Costia* and move more slowly. *Trichodina* and *Trichodinella* are saucer-shaped and have sharp, rasping teeth which damage the surface of the skin or gills when the parasite feeds. *Chilodonella* is a flat, heart-shaped organism. All have numerous bristly hairs called cilia. These parasites can be a severe problem on the skin and gills of fry or growers. They are identified in skin-scrapings by their relatively large size (approx. 5 times that of *Costia*), slow movement and characteristic shapes as revealed in the frontispiece, Fig 11b and Fig 17.

Metazoans
The non-protozoan parasites of salmonids are usually larger

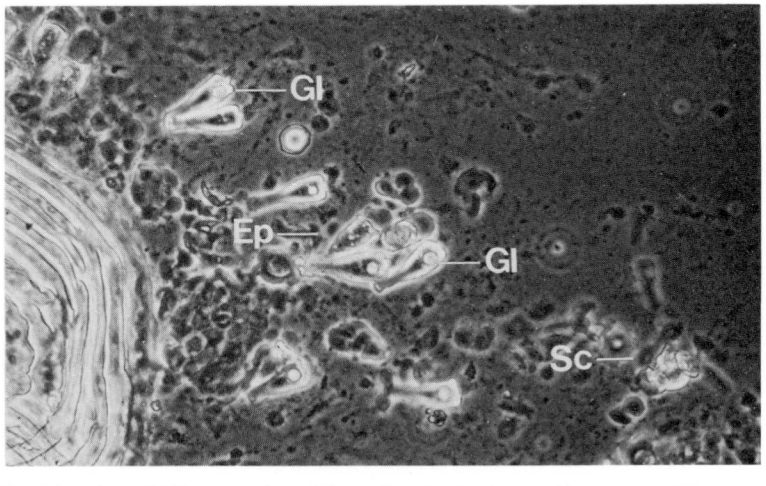

Fig 16   *Scyphidia* complex. These 'suctorian' parasites are readily seen in skin smears of affected fish. The different members of the complex may have stalks, branches, or may be simple vase-shaped structures. Smears containing scyphidians usually also contain considerable cellular débris. (*NB* Gl = *Glossatella*; Sc = *Scyphidia*; Ep = *Epistylis*).

Photograph by courtesy of Mr C H Aldridge.
Copyright, Unilever Research Laboratories.

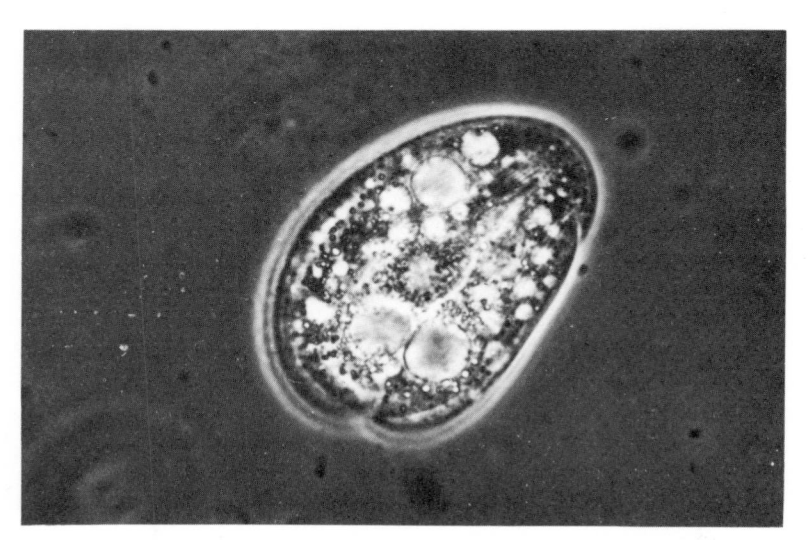

Fig 17   *Chilodonella*. This heart-shaped parasite moves slowly and is readily seen under low power.

Photograph by courtesy of Mr C H Aldridge.
Copyright, Unilever Research Laboratories.

in size, and may be members of any of a wide variety of zoological groups (Fig 8).

Acanthocephalans

The acanthocephalan or 'thorny-headed' worms are very unusual worms, which have no equivalent in higher animals. They have, as the name suggests, considerable numbers of thorny hooks around the head and these are embedded into the lining of the gut. They can cause severe damage, with loss of weight if present in any numbers.

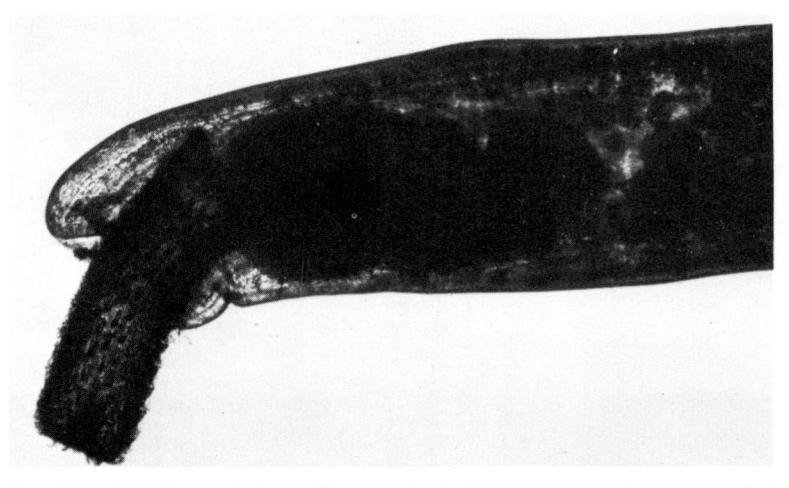

Fig 18 *Acanthocephalus.* The typical thorny head is a rounded structure with arrays of briar-like 'thorns' which are used to attach the worm to the intestinal lining.

The larval stages occur within crustaceans, such as freshwater shrimps, or insects. Severe outbreaks have occurred in fisheries where large numbers of infected shrimps have been introduced in an effort to improve the fish colour or growth rate. The characteristic adult worms (Fig 18) are readily seen with the naked eye in the intestine of affected fish.

Cestodes (Tapeworms)

Tapeworms have complex life cycles involving more than one host. Although varying in length each adult tapeworm has a head (scolex) with suckers or hooks, with which it attaches to the host's intestine, and a series of segments (proglottids) which develop into egg sacs as the tape is extended from above. Tapeworms do not have mouths or intestines, and obtain all their nourishment by diffusion of liquid food across their body wall.

As a proglottid, filled with eggs, reaches the end of the tape, it drops off and is passed in the faeces, releasing its eggs either within the gut or more frequently, when it rots, in the water. The life cycle is continued by the egg being taken up by an intermediate host, usually an insect or crustacean, where it undergoes a stage of development to become a procercoid; then the first host must be eaten by a second host, where a pleurocercoid or infective form is produced. The pleurocercoid's host is then eaten by the worm's final host, where the tapeworm matures into a new egg-producing tapeworm.

There are many variations on this standard fish — tapeworm life cycle. The salmonid may be an intermediate host, where the tapeworm encysts in the muscles or tissues as a pleurocercoid, or it may be the final host containing the worm itself.

1 *Diphyllobothrium*
This tapeworm has its final stage in fish-eating birds such as gulls and herons, the intermediate pleurocercoid being the stage in the salmonid. It occurs in the liver and muscles, especially of rainbow trout, cut-throat trout and grayling.

2 *Eubothrium* spp
This tapeworm is found in a variety of salmonids, both in the wild and in the fish farm. The worms are adult in the salmonid intestine, the intermediate hosts being a crustacean (*Cyclops* spp) and perch which eat the cyclops and develop the parasite to the pleurocercoid stage. Salmonids are infected by feeding on young perch. The adult tapeworm may be several centimetres in length (Fig 19).

3 *Triaenophorus*
This parasite is a problem in almost all waters where pike are plentiful. The pike is the final host, bearing the long white parasites in its intestine for much of the year but only releasing eggs in the spring. These hatch into infectious 'coracidia', which must be eaten by a crustacean within a couple of days. Here they develop into the procercoid and, if the crustacean is eaten by a salmonid (usually trout), they

Fig 19 *Eubothrium.* The tapeworm may be quite long (up to 10 cm) and is shown here attached to the stomach of a trout.

hatch out and migrate to the liver to form the second infectious stage, the pleurocercoid. The final stage of the life cycle depends on the trout being eaten by another pike.

Crustaceans
There are several parasites of salmonids and other fish among the crustaceans—the group containing the familiar lobster and shrimp.

1 *Argulus* (Fish-louse)
Argulus is a crab-like animal capable of living on a variety of fish hosts (Fig 20). It has a very hard coat which enables it to resist predation. It is predominately a parasite of warm, still waters, but can be a problem in trout culture in certain areas. It can easily be seen with the naked eye on any part of the body surface.

2 *Lernaea* (Anchor-worm)
Only the female of this family is parasitic. When mature, it is a leathery, worm-like creature, attached to the muscle of the fish by an anchor-shaped head inserted to a depth of several millimetres. Eggs are released from the female, pass into the water, and undergo a number of maturation stages. Young females are fertilized in the free-swimming stage and then

become parasitic. This entails penetrating the skin of the fish, often at the vent, where the parasite grows its anchor and becomes readily visible (Fig 21).

3 *Lepeophtheirus* (Salmon-louse)

This is a flat, crab-like creature which is normally present in small numbers on wild salmon, but can occur in large numbers under marine farming conditions, It is approximately 4 mm in diameter and the female is readily distinguished by its long, paired egg-sacs (Fig 22). These parasites may usually be seen around the vent or tail of wild salmon, but are often around the head of farmed salmon.

4 *Salmincola* (Gill-maggot etc)

The Gill-maggot is commonly seen on wild Atlantic salmon and sea trout. It does not affect young fish due to its large size. Fresh-run fish therefore are not infected, but once an adult fish has been in fresh water for any length of time, the parasite is usually present. It can persist on the fish when it returns to sea, so that individuals which survive to spawn again almost invariably have severe parasitic damage to their gills (Fig 23). Other species of *Salmincola* have been associated with gill damage in a variety of salmonid hosts.

5 'Others'

A variety of other crustaceans (*eg Ergasilus, Achtheres*) have been reported in salmonids. The gills are the most frequent site of infection.

Nematodes

Nematodes, or 'round-worms', are found in salmonids in many areas but rarely in significant numbers. They usually have indirect life cycles, spending their intermediate stages in insects or crustacea. Their main significance is in spoiling the table value of fish.

1 *Anisakis*

This is a marine nematode which uses salmon, among many other marine fish, as a second intermediate host. The first stage is spent in oceanic krill which are eaten by salmon, where it is usually found in small numbers on the surface of the liver or other viscera. Its final host is normally a porpoise, but it can invade the tissues of the seal or even man. It looks

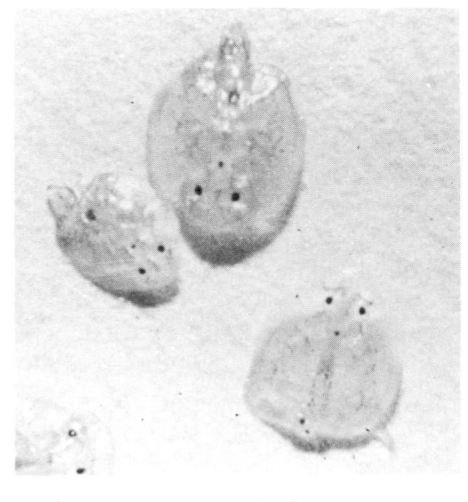

Fig 20   *Argulus*. The 'fish louse' is more commonly found on coarse fish and measures about 5 mm in length. It has a flattened body and a hard skin. It can readily swim from one host to another.

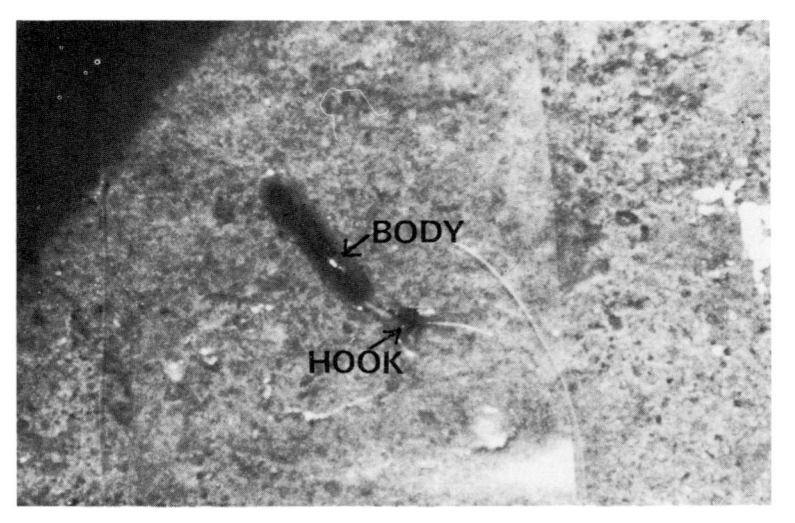

Fig 21   *Lernaea*. Although they are closely related, the 'anchor worm' is different in form from *Argulus*. It has an anterior part consisting mainly of a rigid anchor which attaches to the flesh of the host. Its long fleshy tail protrudes from the fish surface. The parasite takes a long time to grow and it may be found at almost any size up to 1 cm.

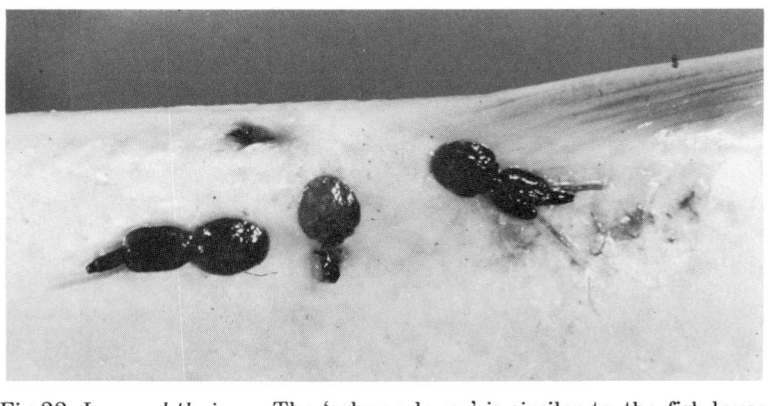

Fig 22 *Lepeophtheirus.* The 'salmon louse' is similar to the fish louse in size and shape but is dark brown in colour and the female has two distinctive light-coloured egg sacs trailing from the rear.

Fig 23 *Salmincola.* The 'gill maggot' is much lighter in colour than the salmon louse and slightly smaller. It is sometimes found in considerable numbers on the edge of the gill margins.

Photograph by courtesy of Mr W M Shearer.

like a small, white coiled watchspring on the surface of the abdominal organs (Fig 24).

2 *Cystidicola*
These are small (about 7 mm) white threadworms, frequently found in the swim-bladder of salmonids. In certain fish, very large numbers may occur but, since they are not found in the muscles and do not usually cause harmful effects, they are of little significance.

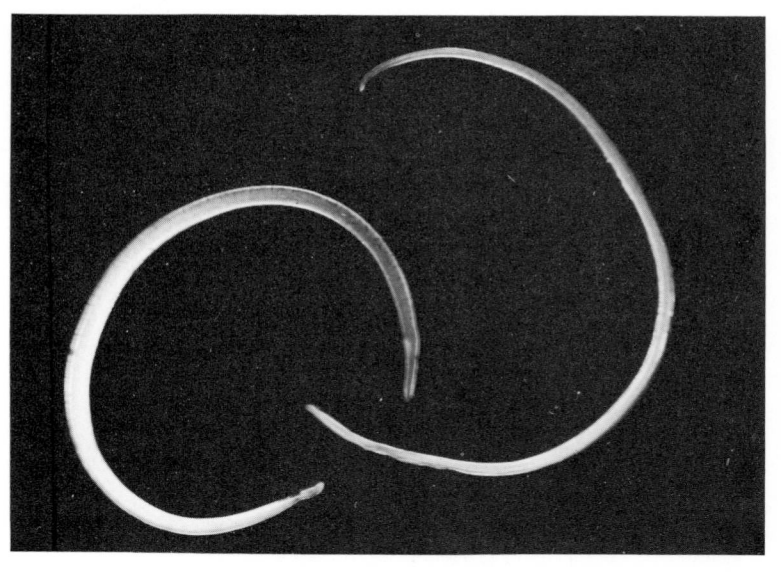

Fig 24 *Anisakis*. These whitish coloured nematode worms are found coiled on the surface of the viscera of marine salmonids. They are around 1 cm in length and may move actively when a fish is gutted.
Photograph by courtesy of Dr K MacKenzie.

3 Filariids
There is a great variety of filariid worms — small red worms found within cysts in muscles or viscera of trout. Usually they are a problem in small lakes where there are large numbers of fish and numerous waterbirds. The worms are very active and will crawl over the viscera immediately the fish is opened.

4 'Others'
Many other nematodes may occasionally be seen in the viscera of salmonids, but are generally of little importance.

Trematodes (Flukes)

Flukes may be divided into two main classes: monogenetic and digenetic. Monogenetic flukes can spend their entire life cycle on one host, whereas digenetic flukes, like tapeworms, require more than one host. The adult flukes are visible to the naked eye.

MONOGENETIC FLUKES

1 *Dactylogyrus*

This is the common parasite of the gills of all salmonids. It destroys gill tissues by means of its suckers and hooks. It can multiply rapidly when there are damaged cells and tissue fluid for it to feed upon. It is up to 1 mm in length and, like other flukes, is best identified (*cf* Fig 25) with a hand-lens or under the low power objective.

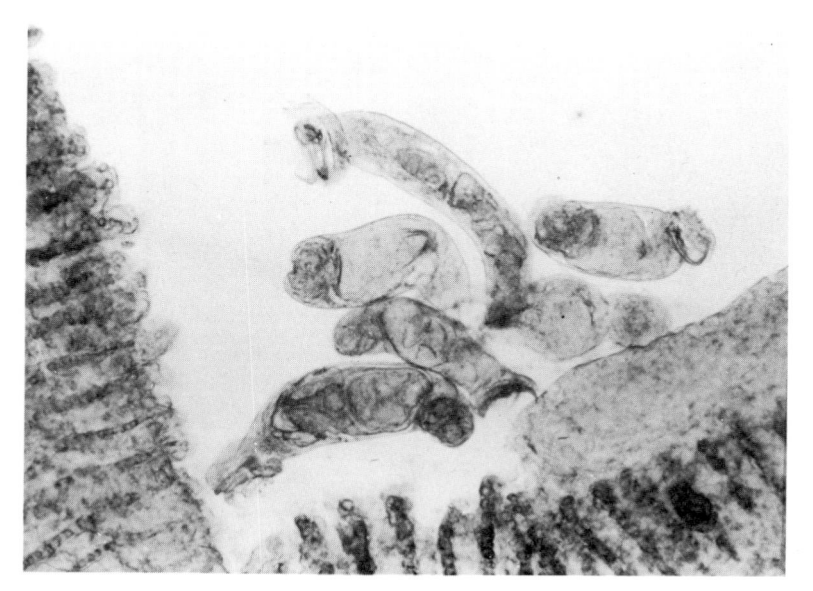

Fig 25 *Gyrodactylus*. The monogenean flukes *Gyrodactylus* and *Dactylogyrus* are usually about 0.5 mm in length and whitish coloured. Readily seen under the low power lens, they are distinguished by their rapid contractile movements. *Gyrodactylus* is viviparous, and in this photograph young parasites can be distinguished within some of the 'parent' parasites.

Photograph by courtesy of Dr R Bootsma.

2 *Diplozoon*

This is a parasite which consists of two flukes fused together. It is occasionally seen in gill preparations and readily identified, but it does not usually occur in sufficient numbers to cause disease.

3 *Discocotyle*

This gill fluke is similar to *Diplozoon*, in that it is larger and less common than *Dactylogyrus* and *Gyrodactylus*. It can be identified by its suckers and its lack of hooks.

4 *Gyrodactylus*

This parasite commonly occurs on the skin, but occasionally affects the eyes or gills. It is viviparous, *ie* gives birth to live offspring, and often a developing embryo can be seen within an unborn embryo (Fig 25). It is readily distinguished by complete absence of the darker spots of other similar flukes, and very conspicuous hooks.

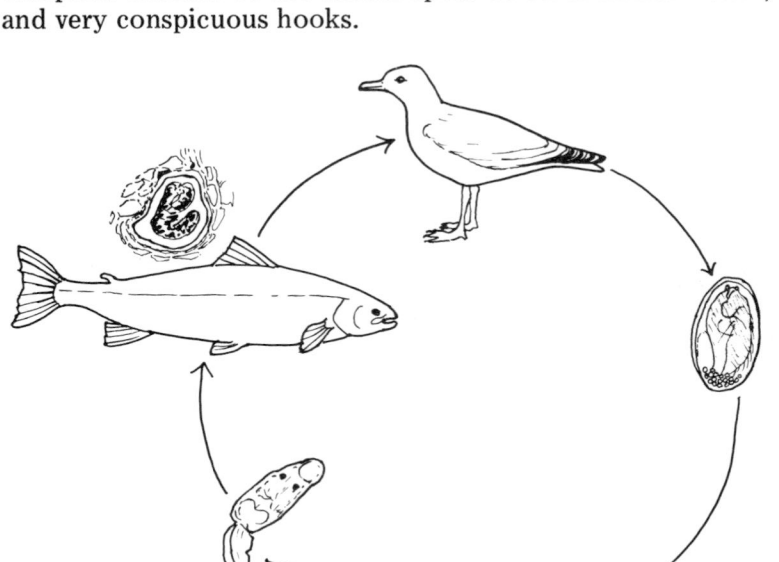

Fig 26   *Cryptocotyle lingua.* The life cycle of this parasite depends on a multiplication stage within winkles (*Littorina littorea*), then release of the cercariae into the water to infect passing fish. The parasite invades the muscle of the fish, to produce a black lesion and must be eaten by a sea bird to complete the life cycle.

DIGENETIC FLUKES

1 *Cotylurus*

An intermediate stage of this parasite occurs in the heart region of a variety of salmonids where it is seen as one or several small white spots (containing metacercariae). Humans cannot act as hosts to this parasite, the presence of which is unsightly but otherwise unimportant.

2 *Cryptocotyle*

This is a very common parasite of marine fish, and is occasionally seen on salmonids in the sea. The life cycle (Fig 26) involves marine birds, which infect whelks (marine 'snails'). In the summer very large numbers of cercariae (Fig 27) are released from the whelks and actively seek and enter fish. Metacercariae are formed in the skin and the host fish lays down a readily visible black capsule around them, hence the name, Black-spot Disease. The life cycle is completed when a bird, seal or occasionally human, eats the fish, and the adult fluke matures within the gut. The metacercaria in the fish is recognized as a small jet-black spot (*ca* 1 mm) within the skin.

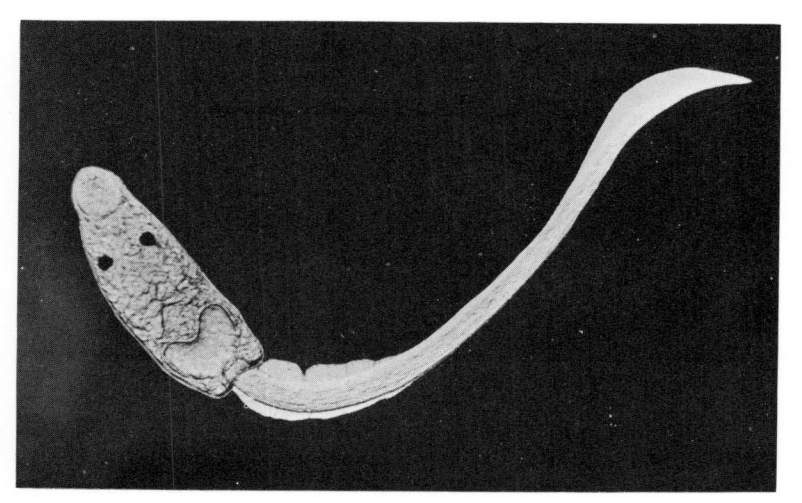

Fig 27 *Cryptocotyle:* cercaria. This is the infective stage for fish. It passes from winkles and, aided by its long tail swims in search of a host. Once it attaches to its fish host, the tail breaks off. The cercaria is small (0.3 mm) and can only be seen in any detail at higher magnifications.

Photograph by courtesy of Dr K MacKenzie.

3 *Diplostomum*

An intermediate stage of this parasite occurs as Eye Fluke within the eyes of salmonids, especially rainbow trout. The life cycle involves the development of parasitic eggs from the faeces of infected water birds into a second stage, which is passed within small snails (*Lymnaea* spp). Large numbers of infective cercariae are released from infected snails in the summer and actively seek and enter the skin of fish. They migrate to the eyes where they encyst in or behind the lens, as metacercariae. The cycle is completed when a fish-eating bird digests the eye and releases the metacercariae, which mature within its gut and produce many eggs (Fig 28). Chopping up the lens of an infected fish and preparation of a wet mount allows identification of the metacercaria (Fig. 29) which can be seen flexing itself.

'Others'

There is a wide range of metazoan parasites which do not conveniently fall into any of the groups already considered.

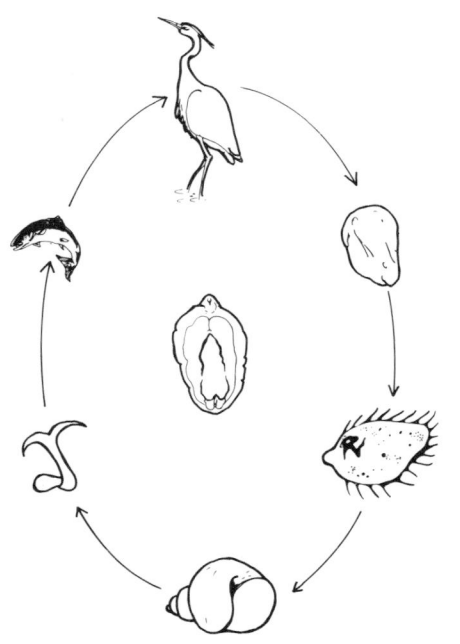

Fig 28 *Diplostomum* life cycle. This life cycle again depends on a snail (*Lymnaea* spp.) and predatory birds, and is the cause of Eye Fluke in salmonids.

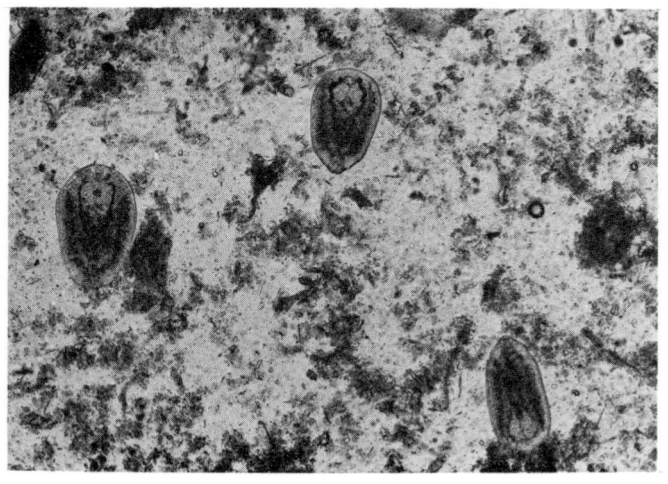

Fig 29 *Diplostomum* spp. This is a smear from the macerated lens of a blind rainbow trout. The metacercarial parasites are readily seen under the low magnification and their bodies can often be seen changing shape.

The three which are most important to salmonids are as follows:

1 Lampreys

The lamprey is a very primitive type of fish which can be a serious problem to salmonids in certain areas, notably the great lakes of North America. It spends most of its life parasitic on other fish, but leaves the host to spawn in a redd, which is not unlike that of a salmon or trout. Lampreys have a large, round sucker at the mouth which allows them to clamp on to the skin of the host and then chew the tissues with their rasping teeth. Lampreys are easily recognized (Fig 30), but show considerable variations in size, the freshwater lampreys being considerably smaller than the marine lamprey, which can be 50 cm in length.

2 Leeches

Leeches are segmented worms which parasitize many animals, including man. They are also parasitic to salmonids and leave the host to breed in summer. They possess suckers at either end of their tube-like body and can loop around the surface of the host by using the suckers alternately. Leeches can swim freely (when they resemble elvers), but if feeding they

65

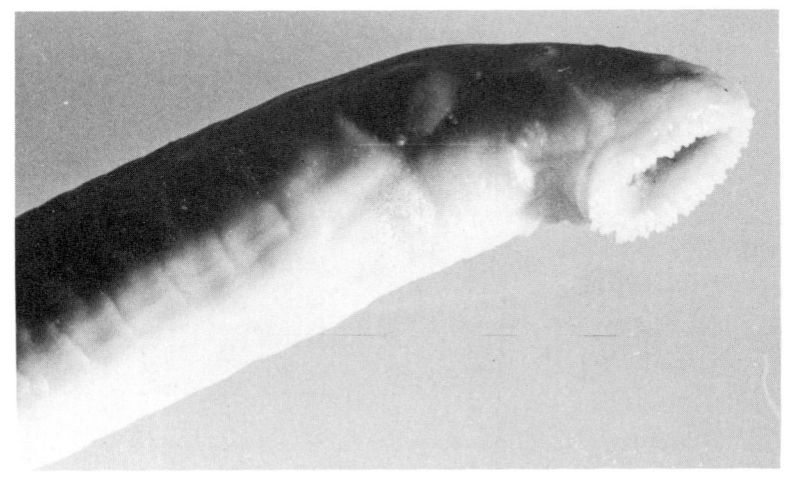

Fig 30 Lamprey. The lampreys are very primitive fish which parasitize higher fish. This example of the river lamprey shows the typical round rasping mouth which grinds its way into the skin and attaches there to feed.

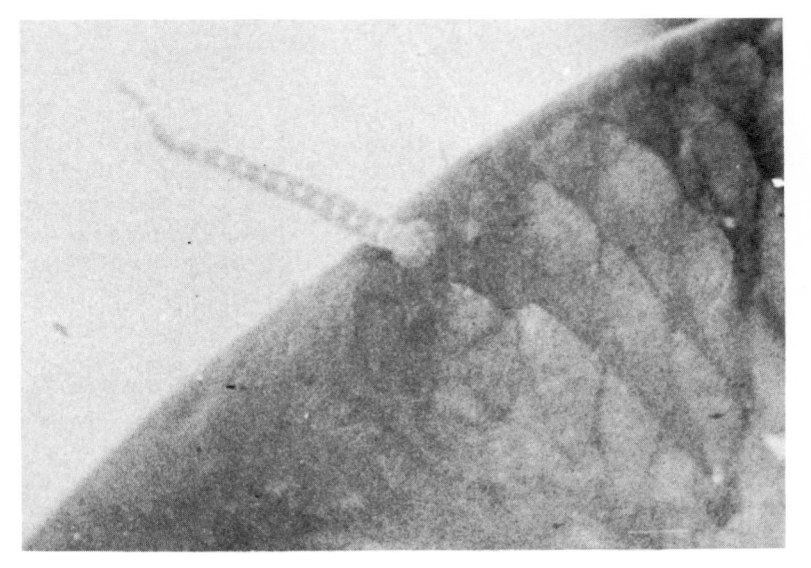

Fig 31 Leech. Leeches are blood-sucking segmented worms. They may be a centimetre or more in length and swim with a looping movement.

Photograph by courtesy of Dr M von Lukowicz.

attach to the skin of the host and suck its blood. They are easily recognized (Fig 31) and measure up to about 5 cm in length.

3 Mussel Glochidia

All salmonids in fresh water are susceptible to infection by the larval form of the freshwater mussel. The larva is expelled by the mussel and must quickly invade the gills of a fish in order to develop further. This involves the parasitic larva biting off a piece of gill, on which it feeds as it enters the underlying tissue. It is then walled-off by the host to form a cyst. These cysts can be identified as white specks on the gill filaments (Fig 32), prior to the release of the next stage and completion of the mussel's life cycle.

Fig 32 *Glochidia* infection. This rainbow trout has many small white cystic structures in the gill lamellae. These are the intermediate stages (Glochidia) of the freshwater mussel.
Photograph by courtesy of Dr T Håstein.

B BACTERIAL DISEASES

Bacteria are very small organisms which can only be seen with the high power lenses of the microscope. They abound in the environment and are capable of multiplying very rapidly. Many bacteria are of considerable value to man and are used, for example, to manufacture certain antibiotics and to produce yogurt. Some are, however, capable of growing in the host, to its detriment. For example, in man, diseases such as tuberculosis, cholera and typhoid are caused by bacteria.

A number of species of bacteria cause disease in fish. They vary greatly in the ease with which they can affect their host. For instance, certain strains of bacteria are capable of killing the host at almost any time, whereas many others can only cause harm at high temperatures, in overcrowded conditions, in very soft water, or in association with some other environmental circumstance which renders the host susceptible.

Some bacteria are normal inhabitants of fish skin or intestinal tract, and when a fish dies, or is killed, they invade the body causing breakdown and rotting of the tissues. This putrefaction occurs very rapidly in fish carcases and is one of the reasons why 'unfixed' material is almost useless for laboratory diagnosis. These bacteria are rarely pathogenic in the living fish, but can complicate bacteriological examinations unless great care is taken.

Outside the laboratory, the only fish bacteria which can be readily seen under the microscope are certain large bacteria which may be identified in wet preparations of gills from diseased fish. However, it is usually necessary to isolate bacteria from fish tissues and grow them within the laboratory for purposes of identification. This can be done using plates of agar jelly which contains bacterial nutrients. The bacteria can also be stained so that they become visible under high power magnification. Since they grow within tissues of the body but not usually within cells, bacterial diseases can often be treated with antibiotics.

The bacteria which are significant pathogens of salmonid fish may be listed as follows:

Table 3 Significant Pathogens

1 *Aeromonas* and *Pseudomonas*
   A. hydrophila
   A. salmonicida
   P. fluorescens

2 *Corynebacteria*
   'Kidney-disease bacterium'

3 *Enterobacteria*
   'Redmouth bacterium'

4 *Haemophilus*
   H. piscium

5 *Mycobacteria* and *Nocardia*
   M. piscium
   N. asteroides

6 *Myxobacteria*
   Flexibacter columnaris
   Cytophaga spp.
   'Others'

7 *Streptomyces*
   S. salmonicida

8 *Vibrio*
   V. anguillarum

68

1 *Aeromonas* and *Pseudomonas*

The *Aeromonas* and *Pseudomonas* bacteria are responsible for a variety of diseases in wild and cultured salmonids. Although some strains are pathogenic at temperatures as low as 5°C, most of these bacteria do not multiply and cause disease at less than 10°C. They damage the host by the action of their toxins *ie* chemical poisons.

(i) *Aeromonas hydrophila* and *Pseudomonas fluorescens*

These bacteria are very common in freshwater, especially where there is a high content of organic matter. They are responsible for identical generalized 'septicaemic' infections of stressed fish, *eg* at high temperatures or spawning.

(ii) *Aeromonas salmonicida*

This is the causative agent of furunculosis — one of the most important diseases of wild and farmed salmonids. This bacterium is different from other aeromanads in that it is only able to survive and multiply within fish tissues. In the laboratory, it is further distinguished from the other aeromonads by a characteristic brown pigment (produced on agar jelly) and also its inability to move in wet smears.

2 *Corynebacteria*

The 'kidney disease bacterium' of salmonids is probably a *Corynebacterium*. It can only multiply within fish tissues where it grows slowly within the kidney causing chronic damage. The organism is more prevalent under conditions of soft water. It is very small and difficult to grow in the laboratory because of its special nutritional requirements.

3 *Enterobacteria*

Although *Enterobacteria* are very common in fresh water, particularly if animal wastes are present, only one member of this group is pathogenic to salmonids — causing 'Redmouth' of rainbow trout in the western USA. Again this organism has not been given a specific name.

4 *Haemophilus*

Haemophilus piscium is the cause of 'Ulcer disease' in Canada and north-east USA. The organism can be carried by symptomless adults.

5 *Mycobacteria* and *Nocardia*

These groups cause chronic infections, such as tuberculosis

and leprosy, in man and other animals. They are characterized by having a waxy coat, which is resistant to destruction either by the natural defences of the host or by disinfectants. *Mycobacterium piscium* causes fish tuberculosis and *Nocardia asteroides* causes similar chronic lesions.

6 Myxobacteria

This group comprises various organisms which are normal inhabitants of water, mud, and the body surface of fish. Certain species can cause specific diseases; however, in general, myxobacteria are opportunist invaders of fish which have become vulnerable because of some stress such as poor water quality or spawning.

    (i) *Flexibacter columnaris*

This myxobacterium is the cause of 'Columnaris Disease', which is so-called because the organism lines up in columns when placed on a microscope slide. It multiplies at high temperatures which is why outbreaks rarely occur below 25°C. It may be readily identified in wet smears at high magnification by the sliding sinuous movements of the organisms as they form into columns (Fig 33).

    (ii) *Cytophaga* spp

This group of myxobacteria are responsible for two conditions which affect salmonids at low temperatures — 'Coldwater disease' and 'Peduncle disease'. The organisms are long and slender (Fig 34), and particularly invade the tail region (caudal peduncle).

    (iii) 'Others'

A variety of myxobacteria are responsible for disease in salmonids under stress. An important example is the colonization of damaged gills by these organisms in the condition known as 'Bacterial gill disease'. In this case, the bacteria may often be identified sticking tenaciously to the gills of affected fish in wet smears at 40× magnifications. Myxobacteria also play a prominent part in other diseases, especially 'Fin rot' and marine conditions such as 'Eroded mouth' and 'Seawater precocity'.

7 Streptomyces

Streptomyces salmonicida has been associated with generalized infections of sockeye salmon on the west coast of the USA.

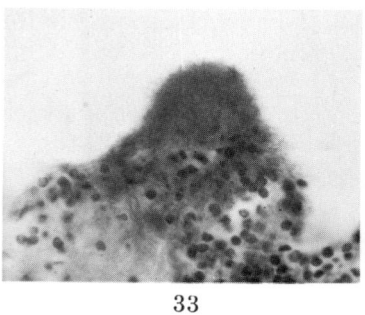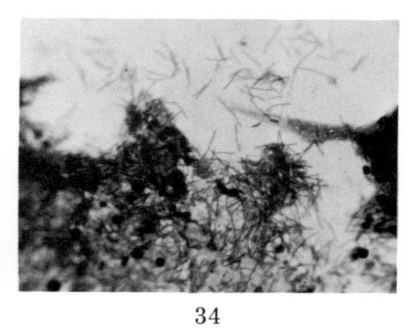

33   34

Fig 33   *Flexibacter columnaris*. The myxobacteria are the only pathogenic bacteria likely to be seen in smears. *Flexibacter columnaris* bacteria, the cause of columnaris disease, move into columns (as in this case) when a piece of infected tissue is placed on a slide. Highest magnifications are required to see the bacteria which appear as shiny sinuously moving rods.

Photograph by courtesy of Dr S F Snieszko.

Fig 34 *Cytophaga*. Another cause of myxobacterial skin disease is the *Cytophaga* myxobacteria. These are similar in size to *Flexibacter* and again the highest magnifications of the microscope are needed to see them properly.

Photograph by courtesy of Dr S F Snieszko.

8 Vibrio

Vibriosis is a disease of almost all species of fish in saltwater and is caused by *Vibrio anguillarum*. This is a comma-shaped bacterium, and eels are particularly susceptible, hence the name. Like aeromonads, vibrios damage the host by the action of their toxins. In human cholera, caused by an organism closely related to *V. anguillarum*, the toxin acts on the gut wall causing dysentery. *V. anguillarum* probably multiplies mainly in the skin of salmonids, but the toxins produced act on the circulating blood cells, causing severe anaemia. This fact can be used to aid laboratory diagnosis, using agar jelly containing blood as a nutrient. Growth of the organism, and hence disease outbreaks, occurs more readily at temperatures above $11°$ C.

C   VIRUS DISEASES

Viruses are the smallest known microbes. They are completely incapable of independent multiplication, unlike bacteria or fungi. They depend for their replication on being able to invade host cells and process those cells into acting as their reproductive machine, so that the host is responsible for producing the virus for its own infection. Cells producing such virus usually die.

Viruses can only be seen in an electron microscope which is capable of enlarging 50,000 times or more. If a full stop (.) was enlarged as much, it would be bigger than a multistorey block. Virus diseases cannot be cured so it is essential that they are controlled by 'preventive' medicine.

There are four viruses known to affect salmonids, but it is very likely that others will be isolated as more knowledge becomes available.

1 Infectious haematopoietic necrosis (IHN)

Infectious haematopoietic necrosis (IHN) is a viral disease of salmonids, which is currently confined to North America and Japan. Originally the group of diseases in wild and farmed Pacific salmon, known as Oregon Sockeye Disease (OSD) and Sacramento River Chinook Disease (SRCD), was thought to differ from IHN of rainbow trout, but now all three are considered to be manifestations of the same disease complex, collectively referred to as IHN.

The virus can be transmitted by contact with infected fish, by feeding on infected carcases. or by exposure to water from an infected source, and it is also carried on the surface of eggs from healthy, infected stock. The disease is not generally observed at temperatures exceeding 15° C, and as with the other virus diseases, identification involves complicated laboratory procedures.

2 Infectious pancreatic necrosis (IPN)

Infectious pancreatic necrosis (IPN) was the first fish virus to be isolated. IPN is endemic in most parts of Northern America, Europe and Japan.

The virus can be carried via eggs, milt, or faeces. Recent evidence also implicates mergansers and seagulls in transmitting it to distant water-courses. The virus damages the intestine and pancreas of affected fish (hence the name), and in healthy carrier fish may be regularly released within various secretions into the water to continue the cycle of infection.

3 Salmon pox

This is probably a virus disease which affects the skin of wild and farmed salmon causing light coloured warts.

72

4 Viral haemorrhagic septicaemia (VHS)

Viral haemorrhagic septicaemia (VHS) is a viral disease, otherwise known as Egtved disease after the Danish village where it was first observed. The causative agent is a bullet-shaped virus similar to that of IHN, although VHS is confined to Europe and affects a different age group. VHS does not survive on the surface of eggs, which facilitates prevention and/or eradication of the disease.

D FUNGAL AND ALGAL DISEASES

Fungi and algae are very primitive plants, of which only a few species are parasitic on salmonids, but they are significant pathogens. Fungi do not contain chlorophyll, the green pigment of higher plants, and are therefore unable to use the energy of the sun, by photosynthesis, to manufacture food.

1 Dinoflagellates

Dinoflagellates are small creatures which are on the border-line between animals and plants, and are probably best classified as algae. Certain members are responsible for major mortalities of marine fish and if salmonids are present, they will also be killed. Death is due to the action of a nerve toxin released by the organisms, particularly when they undergo an occasional population explosion. This phenomenon is known as 'red tide' due to the effect of the body pigments of dinoflagellates on the colour of the sea.

2 *Ichthyophonus*

This fungus is usually found in marine fish but is pathogenic to salmonids, even in freshwater, if they are fed with infected fish. If salmonids ingest the spores of *Ichthyophonus*, the fungus breaks out and can invade all organs of the body. The organism is identified in lesion smears by its characteristic unsegmented hyphae and spore-containing sporangia (Fig 35).

3 *Saprolegnia*

This group comprises a variety of closely related aquatic fungi which are consistently found in freshwater, particularly at low temperatures. They are usually associated with dead tissues and rapidly infect dead eggs of salmon and trout, from which they can spread to live eggs. Living fish are usually

(a)

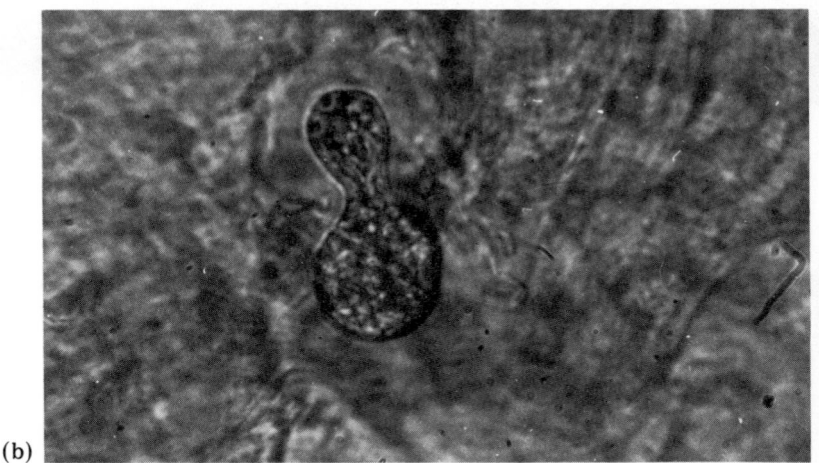

(b)

Fig 35   *Ichthyophonus.* This fungus grows throughout the tissues of infected fish. The fillet (a) shows the whitish sago-like structures in the muscle containing the fungi. The fungus seen in the smear (b) is breaking out of its spore. Low power magnification is usually sufficient to distinguish *Ichthyophonus.*

Photographs by courtesy of Dr J S Buchanan

affected by invasion of *Saprolegnia* through lesions in the body surface and subsequent branching of the fungus over and through the tissues of the fish. The infection is spread by the release of motile spores from the spore-container (sporangium) into the water. Identification is by the characteristic filaments and sporangia in wet smears (Fig 36).

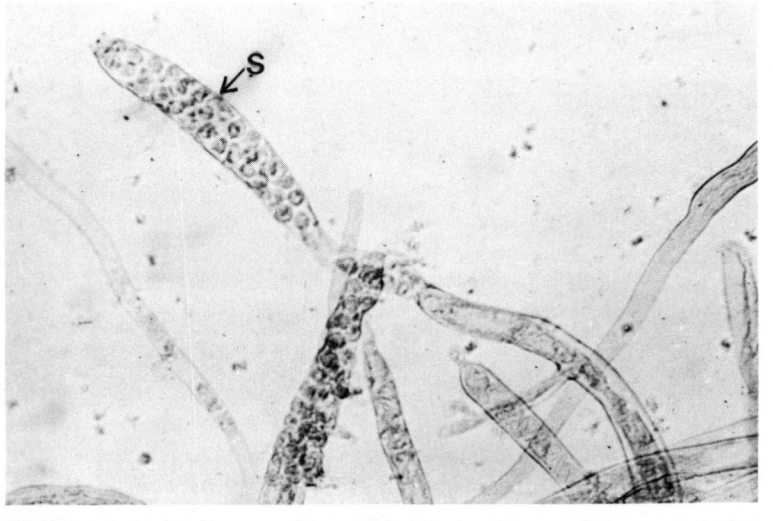

Fig 36 *Saprolegnia parasitica.* This fungus is one of the most serious of fish pathogens. Smears made from the cottonwool-like material, when examined under low power, show the filaments and sporangia (S) containing the motile zoospores which are released and spread the infection to new hosts.

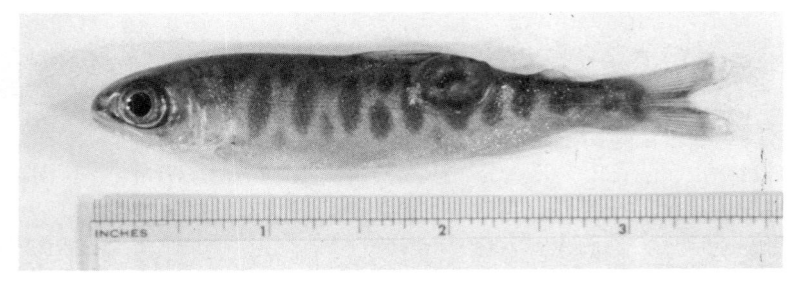

Fig 37 *Scolecobasidium.* This soil fungus occasionally infects the muscle of brook trout and Pacific salmon. The fungus grows within swollen inflamed muscles, and the lesion can be seen on the side of the fish.

Photograph by courtesy of Mr W T Yasutake.

4 *Scolecobasidium*

This fungus is normally found in soil, but it occasionally invades salmonid tissues causing hard raised swellings on the skin or in the kidney (Fig 37). It is a branched fungus with small buds (conidia) containing the infective stages, which can be seen in wet mounts of the affected tissue.

75

Chapter V
Disease Diagnosis on the Farm

Before a fish farmer can hope to diagnose and control disease outbreaks, he must be able to appreciate when his stock is healthy and thriving. This is an art which is only picked up by constant observation and experience. In addition it requires an understanding of how fish behaviour is modified by different conditions. Rainbow trout and brook trout feed much more readily than brown trout and salmon parr, which are more shy. Water temperature, oxygen levels and degree of hunger will all have a potent influence on the eagerness of fish to feed.

Daily inspection of the stock in each pond is an integral part of good husbandry. Before disturbing the fish in a pond, the fish farmer should try to get a good look at them. Without the fish being aware of his presence, he should seek to establish any unusual behaviour and the distribution of the fish throughout the pond. Are they crowded around the inlets or outlets, or scattered around the sides of the pond, or are they fairly evenly distributed as with healthy stock? Are they showing any unusual swimming behaviour, *eg* disorientated swimming, flashing (*ie* twisting over on their sides to give the appearance of a silvery shoal), scraping themselves on the edge of the pond, etc? Having established this, the farmer should approach the pond and watch the reaction of the fish when they first become aware of his presence. Do they 'start' suddenly as if excessively nervous, or do they merely swim rapidly towards him displaying a keen appetite?

Whatever method of feeding is employed, it is essential that the fish be fed by hand at least once a day, preferably first thing in the morning. Eagerness to feed is an important sign of health and should be assessed carefully. Certain disease symptoms are often particularly evident at feeding, *eg* the frantic tail-chasing of trout with Whirling disease. Any obvious signs of sickness should be looked for at this time, especially the presence of gasping fish, dark-coloured or discoloured fish, bulging eyes ('popeye'), eroded tails and fins. This part of the inspection routine is made easier by the use of polaroid glasses which permits a better view of the fish.

The outlet and bottom of the pond should be examined for dead or dying fish which should be removed, counted and buried in lime daily. Occurrence of mortalities following grading is often evidence of poor health, which reduces the ability of the stock to cope with the stress of handling. Several netfulls of fish from each pond should be regularly inspected, particularly if symptoms of possible disease are present. The vigour and conformation of the individual fish should be noted, as well as certain external characteristics:

 (i) the nature of the mucous coating of the skin: is there excessive mucus, and is there any discoloration?

 (ii) the opercula over the gills: are they shortened and, if so, do the gills appear normally coloured (there should be no strands of mucus or fungus visible)?

 (iii) the fins and tail: are they eroded with a ragged edge, or are they intact?

 (iv) any other signs: is there any evidence of a rash or white spots on the skin? Are there any sores, ulcers (*ie* holes), lumps or parasitic animals on the skin? Is the eye normal or does it show popeye, and is the lens clear or cloudy?

If the cause of a particular problem is not immediately obvious, a post-mortem examination may be necessary. For this purpose, live fish, which show frank evidence of disease, should be taken and killed. Dead fish are useless for examination as degenerative changes are evident under the microscope in less than one hour after death and these changes are visible to the naked eye within very few hours. The post-mortem should be undertaken well away from any live fish, and care should be taken to ensure that it is performed hygienically. Thus after the examination is completed, any fish remains should be buried in the lime pit, and the fish farmer should adequately disinfect himself and his utensils (p. 144).

The following equipment is required for a satisfactory fish post-mortem: microscope (see appendix), microscope slides and coverslips, scalpel, mounted needle, fine scissors, hand knife, hand lens, bottles of 10% formal saline. Fish should be killed either by a blow on the skull or by decapitation, and this should be done carefully to avoid removing mucus and possible skin parasites.

(i) Procedure for external examination: Scrape a scalpel blade across the skin surface and place the collected mucus on a glass slide. Add a drop of water and tease out the mucus with a mounted needle. Place a coverslip over the mucus; this is a wet preparation of a skin scraping for examination under the microscope. Remove the gills, or a single gill-arch, with the scalpel or fine scissors (Fig 38) and place onto a slide as before to give a wet preparation of gills. Slit the eye either *in situ* or after dissecting it out of its socket. Remove the lens and associated fluid with a mounted needle. Chop the lens with a scalpel and examine a wet preparation at low power (eye flukes present may also be seen with a hand lens). Any unusual lesions which are visible on the outside of the fish should be dissected free and placed in 10% formal saline if more detailed laboratory examination is required.

(ii) Procedure for internal examination: Slit the fish open along the midline of its belly from between the gills to the anus. Look carefully at the inside of the abdominal cavity and its contents. Make particular note of the colour of the various organs, the presence (and colour) of any fluid present, and also any swellings or unusual lesions, *eg* haemorrhages. Remove the gut and slit along its length with the fine scissors. Smear the contents of the gut onto a slide and make a wet preparation in order to search for any gut parasites, *eg*

Fig 38   Preparation of a smear for a wet mount. (a) The fish is handled very carefully to avoid damage. (b) It is decapitated. (c) The material for examination is carefully removed (in this case the gill, but the process is the same for smears of skin or gut contents). (d) The gill filament is placed on a clean microscope slide (a larger gill would be dissected or teased out prior to examination). (e) A drop of clean saline (or water) is added. (f) A coverslip is placed over the preparation with great care being taken not to include bubbles of air. (g) The preparation is then examined under the microscope. Always examine under low power first, and look for large parasites or the fast movements of smaller ones. This gill preparation is perfectly normal.

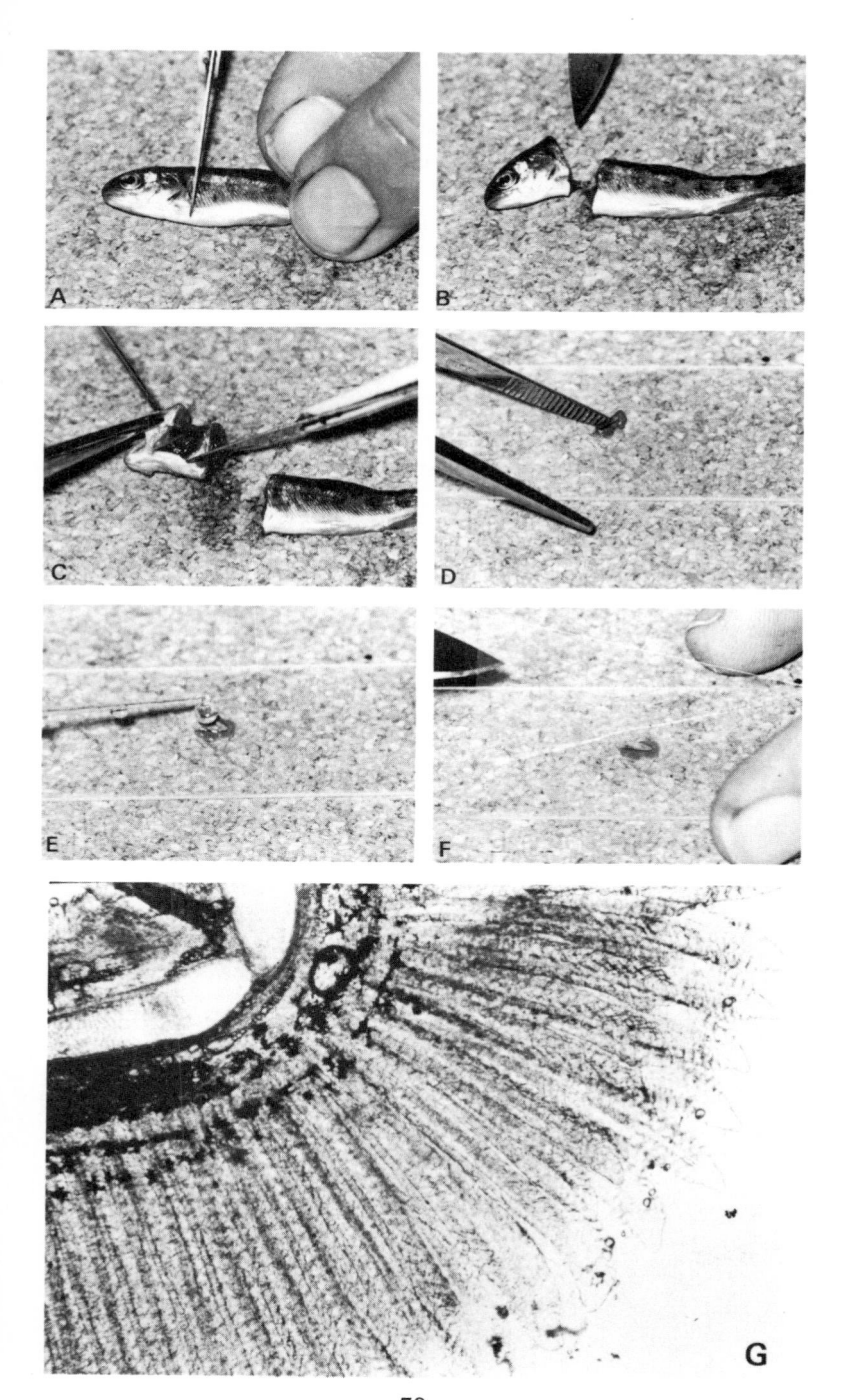

Hexamita. If any unusual lesions are seen with the naked eye, these should also be placed in 10% formal saline for more detailed laboratory examination. Under certain circumstances (*eg* after a fish-kill, or if certain virus diseases are suspected), small blocks of liver, kidney, and gut (at the pyloric caeca) should be removed and placed in formal saline. This preserves the tissues while they are sent to a laboratory for detailed histology which cannot be undertaken by the from one country to another. In the UK, Government laboratories must be notified immediately if fish farmers suspect any of the following diseases to be present: BKD; Columnaris; Furunculosis; IHN; IPN; UDN; VHS; Whirling disease.

Chapter VI
Diseases of Eggs and Sac-fry (Alevins)

In the next four chapters, the important diseases of salmon and trout are described according to the age of the fish. Two particular types of problem are discussed elsewhere — 'Fish kills' and nutritional diseases (Ch X and XI). A fish kill may be defined as a sudden mortality of previously healthy fish which occurs within a period of 24 hours. No infectious disease of salmonids resembles a fish kill, unlike the situation with nutritional diseases. The latter usually appear over a considerable time and may be manifested in a variety of different ways. However, with modern compounded diets, they are probably uncommon and the diagnosis of nutritional disease usually need only be considered as a last resort, unless offals or trash fish diets are used instead of compounded diets.

A DISEASES OF EGGS

A certain number of infertile 'blank' eggs are usually produced by normal broodstock. If more than 20% of a batch of eggs are infertile, then it may be advisable to discard the entire batch.

Apart from those eggs which are initially blank, a certain proportion of live eggs will die before hatching particularly if roughly handled as 'green' eggs before the process of 'eyeing up' occurs (Fig 39). If dead eggs are not removed from the hatchery tray, they will inevitably become infected by fungus which will then spread to adjacent healthy eggs. This may be prevented either by daily removal ('picking') of dead eggs or by regular disinfection using formalin or more preferably malachite green.

Under certain circumstances, eggs may show disorders, notably the occurrence of white and coagulated yolk spots

Fig 39   Dead salmonid eggs. This photograph shows light coloured opaque eggs which have died during incubation. These readily become infected with *Saprolegnia* or other pathogens which can spread to healthy eggs such as the normal (eyed) eggs also present.

inside the egg (and later in the yolk-sac of fry). This is thought to be due to the effects of heavy metals in the water, notably zinc and copper. It is essential therefore, that pipes which are galvanized or made of copper, are excluded from the hatchery. Occasionally eggs will develop a soft and sticky consistency and tend to clump together. Although the cause of these problems is not fully understood, it is thought to be associated with excess ammonia in the water. In this case the best course of action is to increase the water flow through the hatchery and thus flush the ammonia away from the eggs.

It should always be remembered that the quality of the water supply, while extremely important throughout a fish farm, is particularly so as regards the hatchery supply. The water temperature should not exceed 13° C. The water should be free of suspended solids, which will coat and choke the eggs. Disolved iron salts, *eg* from iron pipes or natural deposits, will also precipitate onto the surface of eggs and cause similar losses. If suspended matter is a problem, for example after heavy spates, it may be advisable to incorporate a gravel filter bed at the inlet.

B DISEASES OF SAC-FRY (ALEVINS)
Hygienic hatchery conditions, important before hatching occurs, become crucial after this stage. Egg shells in particular will serve as a focus for the multiplication of fungi and parasites if they are not regularly removed. Attention to sanitary procedures will provide a better environment for the sac-fry, which will thus have a better start in life.

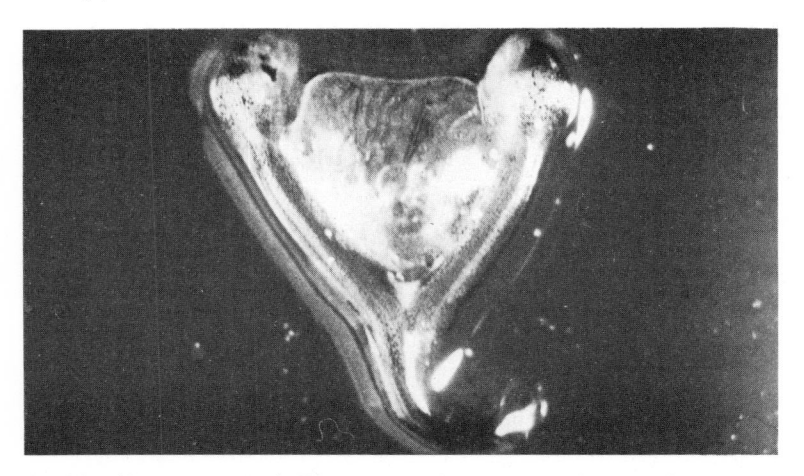

Fig 40 'Siamese twins'. This is one of a number of relatively common congenital anomalies. The two fry are fused at the yolk sac.
Photograph by courtesy of Dr T Håstein.

Very small numbers of abnormally structured fry are not unusual. These 'monsters' may take the form of Siamese twins or the like (Fig 40), and if their incidence is more than 1%, then that particular batch of eggs should be regarded as suspect. Apart from such occurrences, there are two abnormalities of the yolk-sac which are sometimes seen at this stage:

(i) Blue-sac disease
If the yolk-sac increases in size so that the fry cannot swim in

their normal position, then this disease may be suspected. The condition is brought about by an increase in fluid in the yolk-sac which takes on a blue-grey coloration (see Fig 11c frontispiece). The underlying cause is probably the accumulation of metabolic products and the problem is alleviated to some extent by increasing the water flows.

(ii) Deformed yolk-sac
Sometimes it may be noticed that a fat globule within the yolk-sac has become pinched-off so that the yolk-sac itself takes on a dumb-bell appearance (Fig 41). This condition should make one suspect insufficient water flows and/or too high water temperatures for incubation. Increasing the water flow through the system and reducing the stocking density helps in prevention.

Fig 41   Deformed Yolk Sac. A rainbow trout showing a dumbell-shaped yolk sac, a relatively common anomaly associated with build-up of metabolic wastes in the water.
Photograph by courtesy of Dr T Håstein.

Where there is a disease problem of sac-fry with no evidence of yolk-sac deformity, and if both the oxygen levels and flow rate of the water supply are adequate, then the possibility of gas embolism or parasites should be considered:

(iii) Gas bubble disease
Supersaturation of the hatchery water supply with gases can

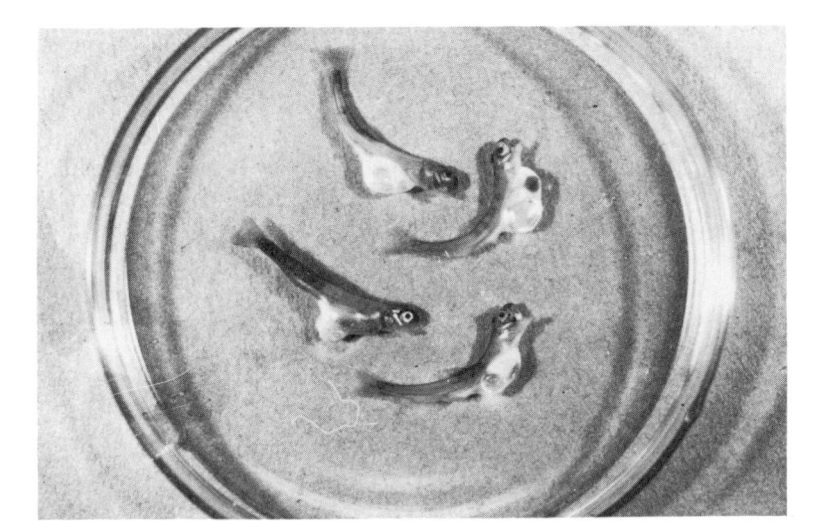

(a)

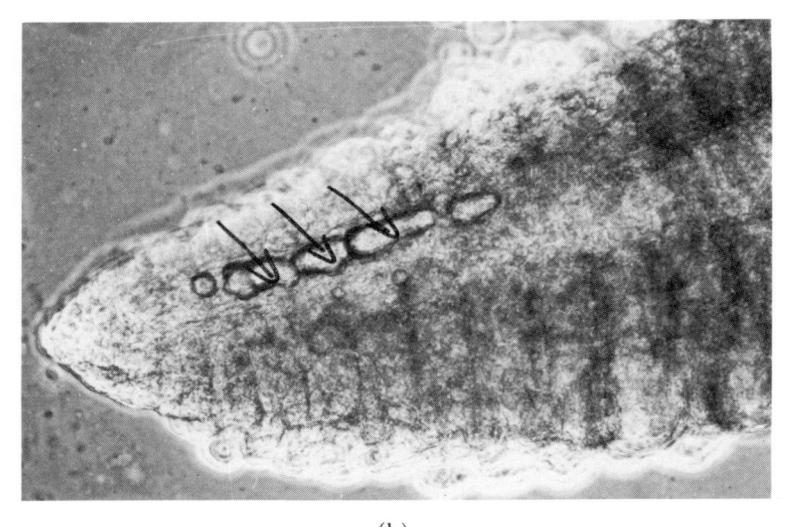

(b)

Fig 42   Gas bubble disease. The site where the bubbles of gas
('emboli') break out of capillaries varies with the age and species of fish.
(a) Gas bubble disease in rainbow trout sac fry. The bubble of gas has
accumulated at the rear of the yolk sac. (b) In young Atlantic salmon
the gill is the commonest site of gas bubble formation. This preparation
shows the tip of the primary gill lamella of a salmon fry. The bubbles
(arrowed) are readily seen in such preparations.

Photograph by courtesy of Mr C H Aldridge.
Copyright, Unilever Research Laboratory.

precipitate a fish-kill among sac-fry (p 129). However, in less severe cases, sac-fry may be found swimming in a disturbed fashion due to the effects of the bubbles of gas within the yolk-sac (Fig 42a). This condition is similar to the 'Bends' which may occur when divers surface too rapidly following a deep dive (*ie* at a high pressure). Affected fry frequently swim upside down or with their heads pointing up vertically, and losses are variable. This condition may be suspected if the fish farmer places his hand in the water and observes bubbles becoming attached to the outside surface of his skin. Bubbles of gas may often appear beneath the skin of individual fish, giving the appearance of lumpy skin. These bubbles may be seen microscopically within the capillaries of the yolk-sac and the gills (Fig 42b), and dying salmon may show no other signs. The remedy is to blow off the excess gas by aeration and/or to repair any leaks in pipelines or pumps which may be causing the problem.

(iv) Costiasis

If daily losses of fry are occurring with no obvious external signs, then parasitic infection should be suspected. *Costia* may sometimes infect yolk-sac fry, and in order to confirm this, wet preparations of skin and gills should be made and examined for this parasite. The problem is treated with formalin (p 150).

Chapter VII Diseases of Early Feeding

First feeding of fry is a crucial stage in any hatchery operation. If undertaken too early, it will encourage infections of the yolk-sac as well as increasing the amount of debris in the hatchery, with all the concomitant problems to which a dirty environment predisposes. On the other hand, young fry which do not get onto the feed sufficiently quickly can live for a considerable period on the food reserves of their yolk and then their body fat. These fish may not seem to be failing, but they become very slender with large heads, *ie* 'pinhead fish' (Fig 43), and then may start to die in considerable numbers. This situation is particularly common when first feeding of Atlantic salmon has been retarded and the fish have gone beyond the point of no return. No matter how much food is available, such fish cannot then make good the early starvation.

The timing of first feeding is thus of great importance and one rule of thumb for trout is that it should take place when

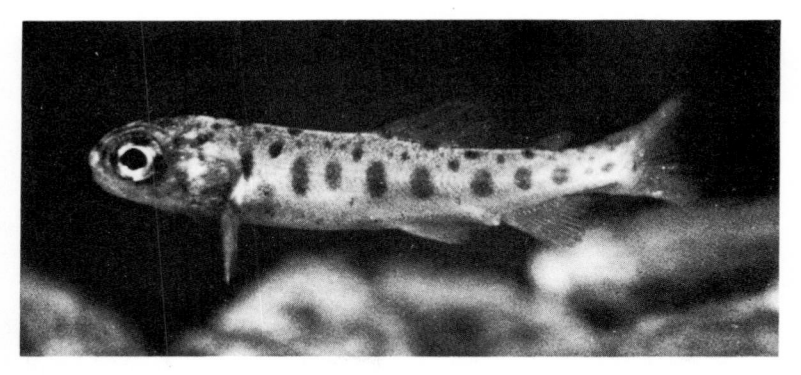

Fig 43   Starvation. Young fish which do not feed get progressively thinner until the head may appear to be disproportionately large when they are referred to as 'pin-heads'.

between 10 and 25% of the fry swim up. With Atlantic salmon the problem is more complicated and one scientist advocates using the ratio of the weight of the yolk-sac to the embryo, *ie* first feeding when the embryo comprises 80% of the dry weight of the whole alevin.

A number of diseases affect fish when they first start feeding. In general it may be said that the younger the fish, the fewer symptoms are seen in any disease problem; the smallest fish simply die. Many of the causes of such loss are living agents, but consideration should first be given to two inportant non-infectious causes:

A STARVATION AND GAS BUBBLE DISEASE

1 Starvation
Even after fry have been successfully brought onto the feed, the hatcheryman may be tempted to underfeed them, being aware of the dangers arising from uneaten food and detritus. However, this runs the risk of starving the fry, which may soon resort to cannibalism, those fish which have never really got onto feed often being the first victims. Large numbers of fish may die in this manner, and individuals often lose their eyes in the initial attack. A fish which apparently has a tail at both ends is sometimes the first evidence of one fish attempting to swallow another. Starvation may be more easily avoided if care is taken to prevent over-stocking and to ensure that the hatchery tanks are cleaned daily. Even if actual fish deaths are not occurring, poor feeding regimes and bad husbandry will increase the number of uneconomical pinheads. As a general maxim it may be said that for first feeders, the more the farmer tries to feed 'little and often', the better.

2 Gas bubble disease
Supersaturation of gases may cause losses among early feeders, as among alevins and older fish. The clinical signs are similar to those shown by alevins, *ie* swimming 'belly-up' or vertically, and often affected fry will be seen to have a bubble of gas in their mouths. Wet preparations of gills will also show evidence of gas bubbles within the blood capillaries and such bubbles may be clearly visible in the fins and tail. Prevention is by aeration of the water supply and careful maintenance of pumps and pipes.

B ACUTE LOSSES

Several infectious diseases of early feeders may cause sudden severe losses. These should not be confused with fish kills, since it is most unlikely that any infectious disease will result in more than 20% of the affected stock succumbing over a period of 24 hours, whereas fish kills frequently cause 100% mortalities within minutes. This sort of situation occurs typically with certain virus diseases and may be called an 'acute' loss. The same organism may, however, have far less dramatic effects under different circumstances, eg where fish are less susceptible because of age or acquired resistance etc. Nevertheless, very young fish are particularly vulnerable, and heavy losses should cause the farmer to suspect one or more of the following conditions:

1 Infectious pancreatic necrosis (IPN)

In a fish farm which has never previously been affected by an outbreak of IPN, the cardinal sign of the disease is the occurrence of high mortality in young fry during the first two months after coming onto the feed. Often losses start to occur about six weeks after first feeding. The affected fry move reluctantly and tend to swim on their sides or with slow spiral movements frequently sinking to the bottom. They may be darker in colour and have swollen bellies (Fig 44). When killed and opened up, there is whitish mucus in the gut and no food present. Occasionally there may also be small blood spots over the stomach area.

The virus responsible for IPN attacks the cells of the digestive system so that both the gut lining and the pancreas

Fig 44   Infectious Pancreatic Necrosis (IPN). Unless fry infected with IPN die very quickly, they often show swelling of the abdomen and darkening of the back.

Photograph by courtesy of Prof N O Christensen.

89

are destroyed. Definite diagnosis can only be made after cell culture and histology. If this disease is suspected, the farmer should place samples of the pyloric area of the stomach from freshly-killed fry into 10% formal saline and send these to the appropriate laboratory, together with frozen specimens or live fish.

No treatment is possible and the farmer has to weigh up for himself the importance of the affected stock to his future programme. It is often advisable to kill out affected stocks (which may all die anyway). The entire fish farm may then be disinfected with an iodophor compound. Ideally live fish should not be moved to another farm, and eggs from fish on an affected farm should not be used for future hatchery purposes.

Adult fish may carry the virus within their organs, particularly the gonads, without showing any evidence of disease. The commonest mode of entry of IPN is in association with eggs brought in from an infected source. Wherever possible such eggs should be accompanied by a Government certificate that the farm has been tested for specific virus diseases. This does not guarantee eggs as virus free (the presence of very few virus particles, undetectable by tests, can still cause disease), but it greatly reduces the risk. In addition it is advisable to disinfect eggs on arrival at the farm (p 144). IPN is a particularly insidious problem as it readily infects wild fish, and while these are not visibly affected, they act as carriers. Such carrier fish can reinfect the farm (*eg* by their excreta entering the inlet pipe), after it has been cleaned out and disinfected.

2 Infectious haematopoietic necrosis (IHN)
This disease is characterized by a sudden rise in mortality, particularly of young fish, under conditions of low water temperature, *ie* less than $10°C$. Affected fish show pale gills, swollen bellies and may trail a ribbon of faeces from the vent. Both Pacific salmon and rainbow trout are susceptible and the disease is at the moment confined to the USA, Canada and Japan. No treatment is possible and diagnosis is by sophisticated laboratory procedures as with IPN.

3 Costiasis
Two parasitic diseases can cause heavy losses of early feeders although neither are usually as sudden or severe as the viral

diseases. *Costia* is a common cause of acute losses in young fish which usually show no other obvious symptoms. This parasite can cause a rapid build-up of infection in a very short time, particularly if water temperatures are rising, the fish are heavily stocked, and the ponds need cleaning. Diagnosis is by identification of the parasite in wet preparations of gills and/or skin. Treatment is by formalin (p 150), and earth ponds which suffer badly with *Costia* should be left fallow for a month in summer after liming.

4 *Hexamita (Octomitus)*

Hexamita often causes chronic low-grade losses (see p 93), but more rarely is the cause of acute losses especially when affecting very small fish. Mortalities do not usually exceed 10% per day and they are associated with a reduction in appetite of the stock and excessive nervousness. Sometimes affected fish show a red vent and a reddened gut when opened up. Diagnosis is by identification of the characteristic parasites in a wet preparation of either yellowish watery gut contents or bile from the gall bladder. Treatment is by Enheptin, Furazolidone or alternative compounds added to the feed (p 156). This is often difficult since affected fish will not be feeding well.

C GILL PROBLEMS

Gill problems are not uncommon among early feeders, particularly where the standard of husbandry is poor. Characteristically such problems are manifested by several symptoms:

(i) continuous minor losses
(ii) fry gathering near the water inlets
(iii) fry 'riding high' on or near the surface of the water
(iv) obvious respiratory distress with gasping and puffed-out gill covers
(v) a high incidence of pinheads contained in poor quality water

These symptoms often follow grading or handling and may be more evident if a netfull of fry is placed in a bucket of water. The two main disease problems involved are 'Bacterial gill disease' and 'Gill fungus', and both may exist together although one usually predominates. The precipitating conditions for these diseases centre around a poor environment such as is brought about by spate conditions or overfeeding, causing a lot of suspended matter in the tanks or ponds. These solids tend to stick to the gill surfaces, and this suffocates the fish or irritates the gill surface and permits disease organisms to gain entrance. A variety of different organisms may be present, notably several species of bacteria (mainly myxobacteria), protozoa (such as *Costia*) and fungi. In conjunction with the poor water quality (low oxygen levels and high ammonia levels), suspended solids and overcrowded conditions, these organisms bring about a disease complex which can arise overnight if fish have been stressed.

Examination of affected fish shows one of two different pictures. In the case of Bacterial gill disease there is a mat of slimy bacteria coating the gills. When a wet preparation of gill material is examined under the 400× magnification, the swollen gill lamellae are obvious and thread-like bacteria are present in large numbers, although individual bacteria may be difficult to see. Protozoan parasites are also seen frequently in association with the bacteria.

If Gill fungus is predominant, the threads of fungus may often be visible to the naked eye. Under the microscope they are very obvious, surrounding and infiltrating the gill lamellae.

As well as trying to improve the environment of the fry, they may be treated by addition to the water of Hyamine 3500 (especially with Bacterial gill disease), copper sulphate, and malachite green (especially with Gill fungus) (p 152).

D   LOW-GRADE LOSSES

The daily occurrence of small losses among early feeders which are being adequately fed is usually due to a variety of mixed infections with external parasites. These parasites infest the skin and gills where they feed and cause irritation, which can sometimes cause symptoms usually associated with older fish, *eg* flashing (p 76). If such fish are examined they often show an increase in mucus secretion and severely affected individuals may show reduced appetite and the appearance of a rash on the sides.

Diagnosis is by identification of the particular parasites in skin scrapings and wet preparations of gills. The commonest parasites seen under these circumstances are (i) *Costia* (ii) the

Trichodina complex, and (iii) the *Scyphidia* complex. Internal parasite infections, particularly with *Octomitus*, are also common under these conditions.

The external parasites may all be treated with formalin. More important, however, is correction of the husbandry faults which have allowed the condition to develop, namely: improvement of water flow rates, decrease in stocking density and the avoidance of undue stress, *ie* excess handling, dusty food, and dirty fry tanks.

Chapter VIII Diseases of Growers

Among the commonest signs of disease is a reduction in appetite, coupled with the presence of fish which are dark in colour, lethargic, and swimming close to the bank or outlet of the pond.

However, certain diseases may be identified by more specific symptoms. For example, aberrations of swimming behaviour may occur in several distinct forms. A disturbance of the swim bladder will cause mechanical interference with buoyancy. Similarly, nervous disorders can upset swimming patterns and cause loss of equilibrium, *eg* in virus diseases and in Whirling disease. Disorientated swimming may be simply due to cataracts and consequent blindness. The presence of skin parasites may provoke irritation and result in curious swimming behaviour, *eg* if the fish attempts to scrape itself on the bottom of the pond, or exhibit 'flashing' as it twists over in the water. These, and various other symptoms, can often help the fish farmer to pinpoint the cause of a particular problem fairly quickly. For this reason a matrix has been constructed (Table 4) which lists 20 of the most significant diseases of growers against their characteristic clinical signs. This matrix should not be regarded as a hard-and-fast set of rules, but may often be used to facilitate diagnosis. It will be seen that some signs, *eg* cataract, whirling, are generally an unequivocal means of identification, whereas others, *eg* inappetance, wasting, are far less specific. Reference should always be made to the detailed description of any condition under the appropriate section of this chapter before any form of diagnosis is made. The diseases of growers are listed under four main sections which are divided up according to the appearance of the disease on the farm. 'Gill problems' and 'skin problems' are self-explanatory; the distinction between 'acute disease' and 'chronic disease' is less obvious. In this text, acute diseases are those which are manifested by a sudden onset and usually spread rapidly throughout a particular stock. Chronic diseases are usually very gradual in onset and are consequently often identified and remedied before the whole stock has become affected. In this case the pattern is similar to 'low-grade losses' of early feeders, although certain chronic diseases may be impossible to treat and can result in severe financial loss.

A   ACUTE DISEASES

1 Non-infectious diseases
As with other age groups of fish, if a problem arises extremely rapidly, the cause is usually non-infectious in origin, as in a fish-kill. Gas-bubble disease will also affect growers with varying degrees of severity, and the signs and remedies are the same as those given previously. A sudden reduction in oxygen levels as may follow a plankton bloom, or a sudden reduction in pH and the presence of plant alkaloids from rotten leaves, following spate conditions, may precipitate a major fish-kill. However, frequently the fish may merely go off feed, and crowd the inlet or sides of the pond in an agitated fashion. The presence of small haemorrhages on the gills may be due to either reduced pH or to leaf toxins. The addition of calcium carbonate to the water will help to buffer any changes in pH.
The 'acuteness' of onset of an infectious disease problem among a population of fish is related both to the speed with which the causative organism can reproduce and to the fitness of the fish. Generally this means that viruses cause the most sudden appearance of disease symptoms, followed by bacteria, and then by parasites and fungi.

2 Virus diseases
Virus diseases can affect susceptible growers in the same way as early-feeders, causing up to 20% losses within 24 hours. There are three main virus diseases likely to occur.

(i) Viral haemorrhagic septicaemia (VHS)
Unlike the other virus diseases of salmonids, VHS usually only affects growers. The disease is a major problem in European trout farms, rainbow trout being very susceptible whereas brown trout appear to be resistant.

Table 4 Matrix showing the important

	Cataract	Dark colour	Flashing	Gasping	Inappetance
IHN					
IPN		+			
VHS		++			
Bacterial septicaemias					+++
Gill problems				+++	+
BKD		+			
PKD		+			
TB/*Nocardia*		+			
Costia			+++		+
Eye fluke	+++	++			
Internal worms					
Large ectoparasites			+		
Hexamita (Octomitus)					++
Trichodina complex			+		
Whirling disease		++			
White spot (Ich)			++		
Fungi					
Fin rot		+			
Gas bubble disease					
Fish kills					

Wasting	Skin ulcers	Swollen belly	Swimming aberrations (excl. flashing)	Skin lesions (excl. ulcers)	Popeye	Motionless and nervous	Mortality	Internal bleeding
							++++	
			++		++		++	
	+			+				
	+			+++				
				+			++	
			+++				+	
				+				
+						+	+	
	+			+				
+		+						
+								
							++	
+		+++					+	
		++					+	
+	+	++			+		+	+
					+++		++	
	++			+			++	+++
		+	++		++		+++	+++
		+	+				+++	+
							+++	++

diagnostic signs of disease among growers

Affected fish generally exceed 5 cm in length, and the main sign is sudden, severe losses, usually associated with haemorrhages in the skin. Fish dying of VHS differ in their pathological features depending on the stage of the outbreak. Fish which are completely susceptible appear very dark in colour and show rapid mortality. The gills are pale with red haemorrhagic spots and haemorrhages may also be seen around the eye-ball. When opened (Fig 45), large blood clots are visible in the body fat, over the gonads and within the muscles. The liver is very pale while the kidney is thinner and bright red.

Fig 45   Viral Haemorrhagic Septicaemia (VHS). This is an example of the acute, haemorrhagic stage. There has been a haemorrhage into the testis and the gills show the pallor associated with consequent anaemia.
Photograph by courtesy of Prof N O Christensen.

After early mortalities in an outbreak showing the acute disease, the picture changes to the chronic form, where mortalities are lower, and fish take longer to die. In this form the fish appear quite black and show severe popeye (Fig 46). They are very anaemic due to the severe internal bleeding they have suffered and this is shown especially in the gills and liver; the swim bladder and kidney may be enlarged or the entire abdomen filled with fluid, producing a swollen, dropsical appearance (Fig 47).

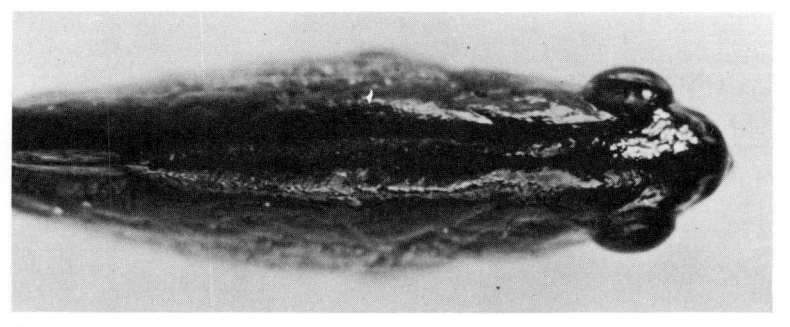

Fig 46   Viral Haemorrhagic Septicaemia (VHS). This specimen is in the chronic stage, with darkened skin and marked pop-eyes due to haemorrhage behind them.

Photograph by courtesy of Dr R Bootsma.

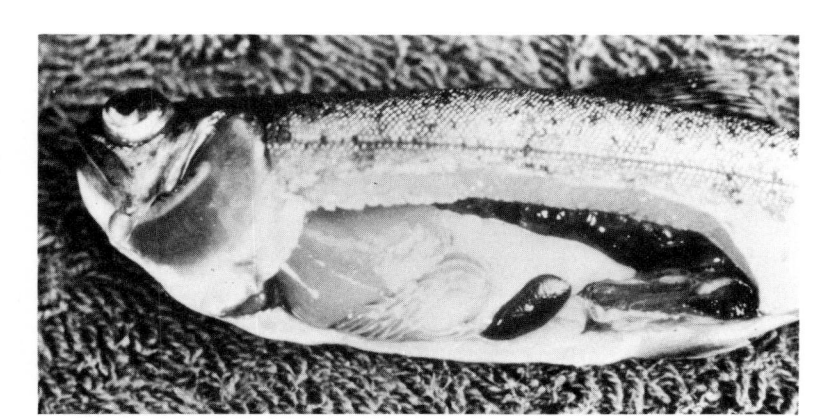

Fig 47   Viral Haemorrhagic Septicaemia (VHS). This is an example of the chronic stage showing the pop-eyes and swollen, grey coloured, nodular kidney.

Photograph by courtesy of Prof N O Christensen.

Towards the end of an outbreak nervous signs appear and affected fish loop the loop with a slow tumbling movement. The presence of haemorrhages throughout the internal organs of salmonids should always make the fish farmer consider the possibility of VHS.

Outbreaks of this disease are most common when water temperatures are at their lowest. Although it has occasionally been reported among fingerlings in summer, the infection usually becomes dormant if the temperature exceeds 8°C. In this case, it will often recur when the temperature drops or the fish are otherwise stressed by handling etc.

Since there is no treatment for any virus diseases, VHS must be prevented from entering a farm by strict control of visitors, elimination of predators, and prior certification of egg and live fish introductions. If an outbreak occurs, it is usually best to kill out the entire farm, leave the ponds fallow and disinfect for three months before restocking with healthy fish. If more than one fish farm exists on the same watercourse, it is usually necessary to maintain a joint programme for prevention and control.

(ii) Infectious pancreatic necrosis (IPN)

Although IPN typically affects early feeders (p 89), it may occur among growers, especially on a farm where the disease has become established. If sudden losses occur when growers are stressed at any time subsequent to an initial outbreak of IPN, then the possibility of a recurrence must be considered. The stress of transporting growers will often bring out the disease the following day ('Travelling IPN'), although grading, or even the onset of sexual maturity may be sufficient. Losses rarely total >20% of the stock and usually cease within four days, but surviving fish may grow poorly. When the guts of fish dying with travelling IPN are opened, they are empty except ˟ a coat of white mucus due to the effect of the virus on the gut lining. In addition, haemorrhages may frequently be seen on the pancreas, stomach and associated intestine. In laboratory diagnosis of IPN infection, isolation of the virus from the gut, sex products or faeces of infected carriers (*eg* broodstock) is made far easier if they have been transported or crowded immediately prior to testing.

(iii) Infectious haematopoietic necrosis (IHN)

The occurrence of IHN among growers follows the same pattern and should be dealt with in the same way as described for early feeders (p 90). It occurs at low water temperatures and is typified by sudden losses of fish which trail faeces from the vent and often show popeye, pale gills and swollen abdomens. When fish are opened, they show haemorrhages over the stomach area (Fig 48) which are more obvious than those which occur with early feeders (*cf* IPN).

3 Bacterial diseases

Like viruses, bacteria may precipitate severe losses but the onset is not quite so sudden. The fish invariably go off feed

Fig 48   Infectious Haematopoietic Necrosis (IHN). Although pre-dominantly a disease of very young salmonids and affecting the kidney and spleen, the virus of IHN also affects the pancreatic tissue as can be seen in the pinpoint haemorrhages on this specimen (*cf* IPN).

Photograph by courtesy of Dr T Kimura.

1-2 days before they start to die. These diseases mostly occur at high water temperatures and sudden inappetance under these circumstances often means that the farmer has to diagnose and treat the fish urgently or severe losses will ensue.

(i) Furunculosis
This disease is caused by *Aeromonas salmonicida* and is characteristically a problem when water temperatures are at their peak. After a brief period of reduced feeding, fish will sometimes die due to furunculosis without showing any other signs at all. This is a particularly common pattern with small trout and Atlantic salmon parr, and can only be diagnosed with certainty by laboratory evidence of the bacterial colonies in the kidney and other organs.

In older fish, the disease is more easily identified by the frequent presence of 'furuncles'. These are large red swollen boil-like lesions, which give the disease its name and are usually found over the shoulder or back, (Fig 11d) (see frontispiece). These burst and release reddish fluid containing large numbers of bacteria which rapidly spread the infection.

The bacterium involved persists in small numbers between outbreaks of the disease within the tissues of a few fish on

101

the farm, or in wild fish in the watershed. The disease is more common in salmon and brown trout than in rainbow trout. However, provided that affected fish can be persuaded to eat sufficient medicated food, all species can be treated by addition to the feed of various drugs. The best drugs for this disease are sulphonamides and antibiotics, notably sulphamerazine and oxytetracycline (see p 156).

(ii) Other bacterial septicaemias

Apart from furunculosis, the *Aeromonas* and *Pseudomonas* bacteria are responsible for a variety of diseases in wild and cultured salmonids. In summer the diseases occur when water temperatures are high and there is a large amount of organic material present. Usually only a few fish are affected and the characteristic features are bright red blotches around the vent, back and sides. When opened up, such fish show haemorrhages throughout the internal organs and the kidney appears completely liquefied.

A similar problem can occur later in the year and is called 'Autumn aeromonad' disease (p 134). All of these infections may be treated by the use of antibiotics or sulphonamides in the feed provided that the fish will eat sufficiently (p 156).

(iii) Botulinum disease

Clostridium botulinum is notorious for being a very occasional cause of death in man and animals which eat rotten food containing its toxin (p 128). However, it has been recently reported as causing death in trout which are given wet fish diets in the summer. If the diet is not fed fresh under these circumstances, it may decompose and *Clostridium botulinum*, present in the trash fish, may form its toxin. Ingestion of the toxin by trout causes them to lose equilibrium and sink to the bottom. They jerk themselves back to the surface again, but sink repeatedly and die within a few hours. This problem has caused severe losses on some Danish trout farms where it has been called 'Bankruptcy disease'. Prevention is by avoiding the use of food which is not fresh and by regular disposal of any dead fish.

4 Parasitic diseases

A number of parasitic diseases of growers can arise very quickly, particularly infections of the skin. Generally parasites cause reduction in appetite and signs of skin irritation or gill trouble. However, certain parasites can occasionally cause sudden losses without much prior warning. The parasites which may fall into this category are *Myxosoma, Ichthyophthirius* and *Hexamita.* Acute parasite infections, with the first two organisms, cause losses which may be associated with either frantic whirling movements *(Myxosoma)* or severe skin irritation, with white skin spots and attempts by the fish to scrape themselves on the banks *(Ichthyophthirius).*

(i) Whirling disease
The fast whirling movements which give this disease its name are caused by the spores of *Myxosoma cerebralis,* and are quite characteristic. The spores of this parasite enter the cartilage of young salmonids, particularly rainbow trout, and cause a severe reaction when it changes to bone. In trout, cartilage becomes bone when the fish reach 6-8 cm in length and massive infections will occasionally result in severe mortalities at this stage. More commonly fish survive but show chronic damage. The spores damage the balance organ which causes whirling, and also press on the spinal column, which causes deformities of the back and tail and dark coloration (Fig 49).

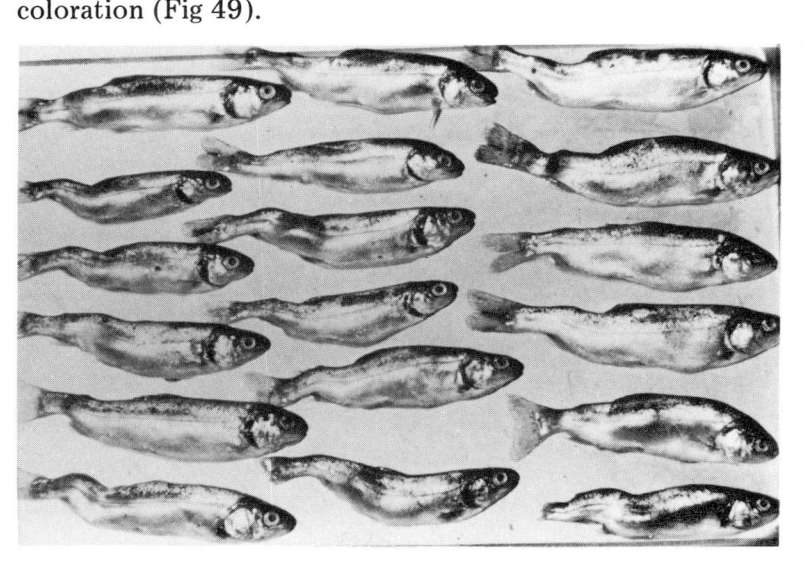

Fig 49   Whirling disease. These fish have all suffered skeletal deformity as a result of the activity of *Myxosoma cerebralis* parasites.
Photograph by courtesy of Prof N O Christensen.

If Whirling disease is suspected on the basis of these clinical signs, microscopic identification of the spores may be attempted. After decapitation of affected fish, the hardening cartilages of the skull should be scraped onto a slide. A wet preparation may then be made and examined under 40×️ magnification. Presence of the small shiny spores (Fig 13) will give a positive diagnosis but several fish may require to be examined.

This disease is prevented by rearing fish in water which is free of spores, *eg* spring water. If this cannot be done, then the use of concrete or fibreglass rearing tanks instead of earth ponds will minimize the chances of infection. Once their bones have hardened, salmonids are resistant to the signs of infection and can then be placed in earth ponds without risk.

(ii) White-spot (Ich)

Acute infections with *Ichthyophthirius* can occasionally cause sudden losses in salmon and trout under conditions of high water temperature and low flow rates. Affected fish show extreme skin irritation and may jump all over the pond as if short of oxygen. They often scrape themselves along the bottom and sides of the pond and may be seen flashing. Examination of such fish usually shows the presence of small white parasites in the skin (Fig 50). Skin scrapings of affected

Fig 50   White Spot or 'Ich'. *Ichthyophthirius* infection produces small raised whitish spots such as can be seen on this rainbow trout. Smears taken from such lesions show the characteristic parasites seen in Fig 11a.

fish should show both the small rapidly revolving infective stage and the large brown adult with its horseshoe-shaped nucleus (Fig 11a).

Ich parasites thrive in conditions of dirty water, low flow rates and dusty feed. Prevention should aim at good husbandry conditions. Treatment is either by formalin or more preferably by a mixture of formalin and malachite green (p 151).

(iii) *Hexamita (Octomitus)*

Unlike the other two parasitic diseases, infection with *Hexamita* often does not show distinctive signs other than a sudden increase in losses. The parasite is in the intestine where it causes haemorrhage which may sometimes result in an obviously reddened gut and vent. Mortalities do not usually exceed 10% per day and the stock may show excessive nervousness and go off their food. Less affected fish are dull, often dark-coloured and have a reduced appetite.

When the intestine of such fish is opened it may contain a clear or yellowish fluid (*cf* IPN) in wet preparations of which the parasites may be seen (Fig 14). Treatment is by Enheptin, Furozolidone or other compounds in the feed (p 156). The main problem is adequate medication of affected stock due to the reduction in appetite.

B SKIN PROBLEMS

The external surface of fish includes parts of the gills and the eye and is often a very good indication of the state of health. Fish which are unwell are less able to resist invasion of the external surfaces by various parasites and fungi. Some viral and bacterial infections are also manifested by changes in the skin of the host.

Once again one may broadly divide the diseases affecting the skin into two main groups: those which result in a sudden acute problem and those which cause a chronic problem.

1 Acute skin problems

The vast majority of acute skin problems in salmonids are due to external parasite infections. These irritate the fish which may respond in a variety of different ways.

(i) Flashing

This is a very common phenomenon among growers and

describes the situation when one or more of a group of fish suddenly make a rapid movement on their sides momentarily giving a silvery appearance under the water. This sign, when repeated, should encourage the farmer to examine several netfulls of fish. If these show evidence of an increase in mucus secretion (often blue-grey in colour) and the presence of irregular pale patches on the skin, then the cause is likely to be an external parasitic infection. Often, however, such fish may flash without other signs, apart from a slight reduction in appetite. In these cases, it is necessary to make a wet preparation of several skin scrapings. Microscopical examination at 40× magnification will permit identification of the commonest cause — *Costia*. Lower power observation (10×) will permit differentiation between the other main causes of flashing. In order of increasing size, these comprise the organisms of the *Trichodina* complex, of the *Scyphidia* complex, *Ichthyophthirius* and *Gyrodactylus*. The last two usually cause other signs and are described in the next section. *Scyphidia* causes only mild irritation, but heavy *Trichodina* infections may cause a rash on the skin (Fig 51). Affected fish in this condition may be seen swimming up to the surface and then dropping down to the bottom apparently lifeless (similar to fish with Botulinum disease, but resulting in much smaller losses).

Fig 51   External parasitism. *Trichodina* have caused this lesion on the back of an Atlantic salmon. The whitish patch (arrowed) is a mixture of parasites, tenacious mucus and skin cells.

External parasitic infections are most commonly seen in ponds with a low water exchange rate. These parasites thrive in conditions of poor water quality, especially if the fish are overstocked and there is a lot of suspended matter present in the water, *eg* due to dusty feed. Thus control measures should include rigorous attempts to improve the husbandry conditions, *eg* by thinning out the stock in the ponds. However, some skin parasites, notably *Costia*, will sometimes cause trouble even when conditions are excellent. In these cases, it is necessary to use a formalin treatment, given as a flush or more preferably a bath (p 150).

(ii) Scraping

In certain types of severe skin irritation, affected fish may be seen to scrape themselves along the bottom or bank of the pond. Such fish frequently show other signs such as flashing, jumping at the inflow, reduced appetite, and varying degrees of mortality. This combination of signs is invariably due to one or more of the following parasites: *Ichthyophthirius*, *Gyrodactylus*, *Lernaea*, and *Argulus*.

All four conditions are fairly easily identified without the need for microscopy. *Ichthyophthirius* is a particular problem under conditions of high water temperature and usually causes 'pustules' on the skin. *Gyrodactylus* may be recognized as its worm-like body changes shape on the fish or after transfer to a microscope slide. *Lernaea* usually inserts its anchor at the base of a fin or in the vent area, while *Argulus* moves rapidly around the fish and will often swim away as soon as affected fish are netted out for examination.

As with other external parasites, the first condition of effective control is to eliminate the environmental factors which predispose to the problem. However, all four infections may be treated by the addition to the pond of various chemicals. *Ichthyophthirius* is best treated by a mixture of formalin and malachite green or as with *Gyrodactylus* by formalin alone; *Lernaea* and *Argulus* by organophosphorous compounds such as Masoten (p 152). In addition, it is advisable to leave badly affected ponds fallow for a month after ploughing in quicklime. This is best done in summer and may also be of use when *Costia* is a problem.

(iii) Others

A variety of other acute conditions can affect the skin. Predators, such as herons, frequently damage fish, causing wounds and ulcers which may become secondarily infected with bacteria and fungi. Ulcers and haemorrhages may be due to acute bacterial infections such as Cold water disease or, in summer—furunculosis. Virus diseases, *eg* VHS, can cause skin haemorrhages but one such disease, Salmon Pox, causes proliferation of warts over the skin surface. Finally, sunburn can traumatize the back of the fish and cause the dorsal fin to shrivel; this frequently happens in heavily-stocked raceways (Fig 52), but also occasionally in the wild (p 140).

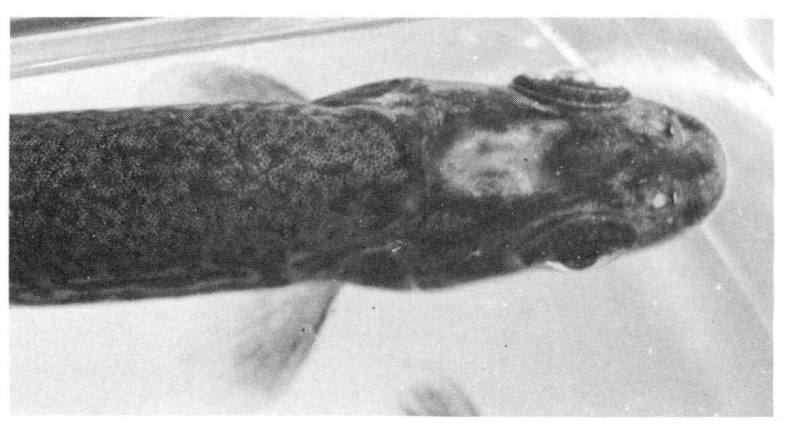

Fig 52   Bald Spot. Sunburn lesion in American lake trout (*Salvelinus namaycush*).

Photograph by courtesy of Dr L N Allison.

2 Chronic skin problems

Many of the acute skin problems, if permitted to continue will cause the fish to become increasingly emaciated and under-nourished. Such fish are usually dark in colour and lethargic. The skin of these fish initially secretes excess mucus. Later, however, it becomes rough, discoloured, and readily invaded by other organisms, especially fungi.

A frequent occurrence, particularly under conditions of poor husbandry, is that of fish with eroded tails and fins. At first, the fins merely show a ragged edge (Fig 53), but gradually they become progressively more eroded. At this stage bacterial and fungal colonies have usually become established and they extend the process into healthy tissue which subsequently dies. Eventually the infection becomes generalized resulting in death. It is no use simply to kill off

Fig 53   Fin Rot. This myxobacterial lesion depends on some pre-disposing factor such as overcrowding, dietary imbalance or poor water quality.

these organisms in order to reduce the incidence of 'Fin Rot' and 'Peduncle Disease' (Fig 54). The disease process is primarily due to the response of the fish to an insanitary environment, sometimes complicated by an unbalanced diet. Adequate water flows and clean ponds, which are not overstocked, will prevent these problems becoming significant.

C   GILL PROBLEMS

Gill problems are not nearly so much of a problem in growers as among very young fish. However, poor husbandry, which is usually manifested by skin problems, will also increase the incidence of gill diseases. Skin parasites and related organisms, will often colonize the gills and such fish may

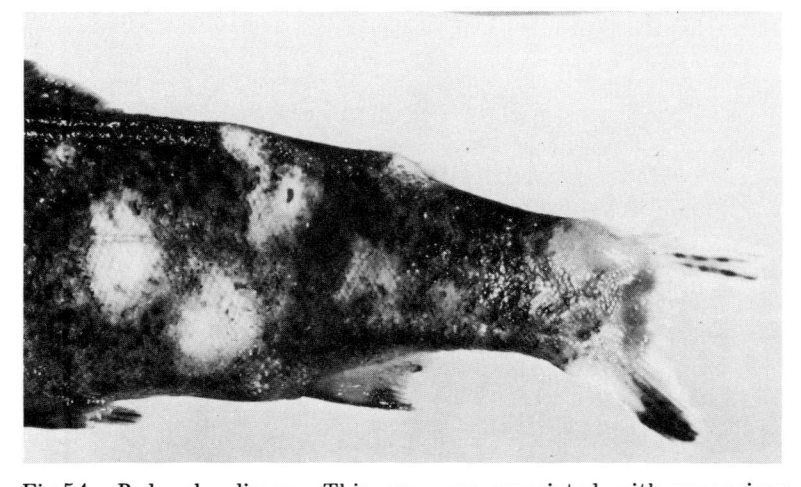

Fig 54 Peduncle disease. This case was associated with precocious sexual maturity in fish held in salt water. The tail has become infected with myxobacteria, but in fresh water the same condition often predisposes also to *Saprolegnia*.

show obvious signs of respiratory distress. In these circumstances, affected fish tend to crowd the inlets and show extended gill covers, and rapid gasping. Such fish usually have a reduced appetite and suffer variable losses, particularly when water temperatures are high. For accurate diagnosis, a wet mount of the gills of affected fish should be examined. The commonest causes of such problems are small ectoparasites (*eg Costia*), gill flukes (notably *Dactylogyrus*), and various myxobacteria. However, the primary cause is the poor environment. Therefore the use of formalin (against *Costia* and gill flukes) or Hyamine 3500 (against myxobacteria) without appropriate correction of the husbandry conditions is at best a short term measure, and at worst the extra stress which finally kills the whole stock in a pond. If gill problems are significant under conditions of satisfactory husbandry, a careful check should be made on the water chemistry. The presence of certain effluents, notably suspended solids and dissolved heavy metals, will provoke severe gill problems and abundant mucus production. This situation may not cause concern when water temperature is low and flow rates are high. However, when the temperature increases with consequent reduction in dissolved oxygen levels, such hidden problems may suddenly worsen the already inadequate gill function, causing severe stress and even heavy losses.

D CHRONIC DISEASES

If a population of fish survives an acute outbreak of disease, frequently a proportion will become chronically affected. Thus fish which have survived an initial outbreak of Whirling disease will continue to exhibit the symptoms of infection. Carrier fish which have survived an outbreak of IPN virus are usually vulnerable to the stress of grading or transport. With VHS disease, the appearance of nervous signs indicates that the acute phase of the infection has given way to a chronic phase. In this case the chronic disease state heralds the end of the disease outbreak. In the case of certain diseases, however, the infection is essentially a chronic process from the start. Human tuberculosis and leprosy are examples of such chronic infections and similar infections occur in fish. In this section, chronic diseases are divided into these specific diseases and into a group called 'bad-doers'. The latter embraces the various types of chronically diseased fish which are a common occurrence on many fish farms. Their poor state of health is usually evident over a considerable time and can have a variety of causes.

1 Chronic infections

Certain chronic infections such as Whirling disease and Fin Rot have been discussed earlier. Of the remainder, four specific diseases will be discussed. Only one ('Eye fluke') is very common and easily distinguished by the cataracts it causes; the other three are less common and affected fish usually show body swellings.

(i) Eye fluke

Fish with Eye fluke *(Diplostomum)* infection show a whitish opacity or white specks in one or both eyes, and varying degrees of blindness. (Fig 55). They are usually dark-coloured and often swim at the sides of the pond, where they are easy prey for predatory birds.

The parasitic life cycle involves snails and fish-eating birds. It may be broken by the use of molluscicides against the snails, notably Frescon or copper sulphate (p 154). Electric grids may be placed across the water inlet in an attempt to kill off the infectious stages after they have left the snail. The use of predator netting, bird scarers etc will discourage birds from either eating infected fish or transmitting infection to the farm in their faeces. Diagnosis can be confirmed by microscopic examination of a smear of the macerated lens (Fig 56).

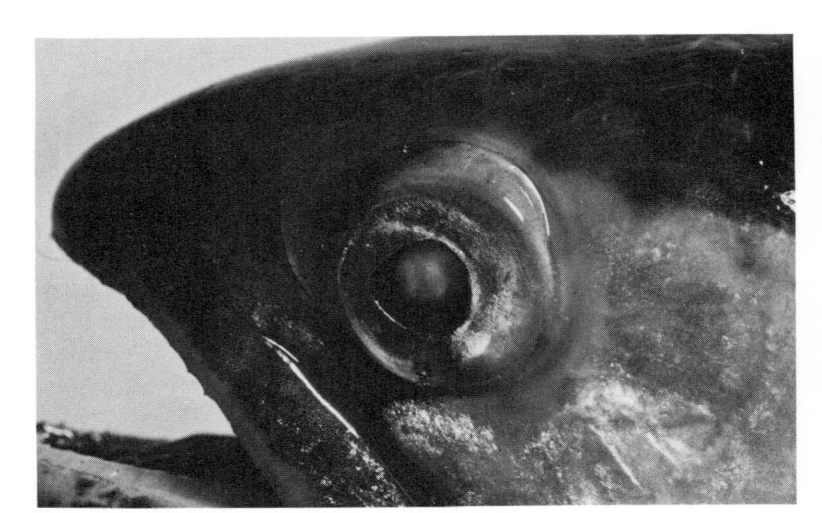

Fig 55   Eye Fluke. A cataract, or opacity of the lens can be seen through the pupil, and is due to parasitic infection with *Diplostomum*.

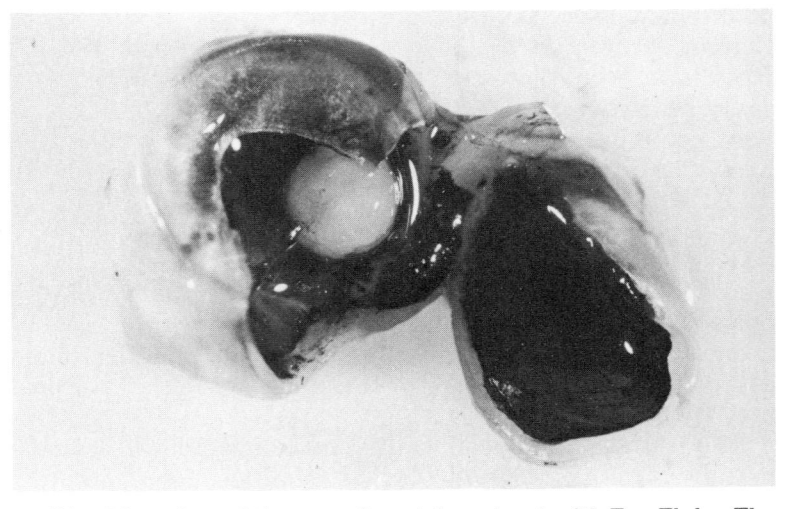

Fig 56   Dissection of the eye of a rainbow trout with Eye Fluke. The lens is obvious as a white ball bathed in fluid. When it is chopped up and made into a smear preparation, the parasites may be seen (Fig 29).

(ii) Tuberculosis (TB)

Infections with either *Mycobacterium tuberculosis* or *Nocardia* bacteria are the cause of swellings in the head and abdominal regions together with generalized wasting. The disease can affect whole stocks of fish which will initially show a reduction in conversion efficiency and then gradual development of lumps on the body and increased losses (Fig 57). If affected fish are cut open, they will usually show either one large white lump or lots of small white specks scattered throughout the body (Fig 58).

Fig 57   *Nocardia* infection in Pacific salmon. The swellings produced by this bacterial disease, known as granulomas, are found in the mouth or abdomen and produce severe deformity.

Photograph by courtesy of Prof R D Wolke.

Fig 58   *Nocardia.* At post-mortem, the whitish structures containing the bacteria are seen. The lesions are very similar to those of *Streptomyces* and tuberculosis infection.

Photograph by courtesy of Dr S F Snieszko.

This disease is commonly associated with the feeding of trash fish or fish offals. Severe outbreaks have occurred when viscera from salmon and trout have been fed back to the fish without prior pasteurization. Treatment is usually not feasible and control is by changing the method of food preparation.

(iii) Bacterial kidney disease (BKD)

The occurrence of spasmodic mortalities in association with an overall reduction in growth and conversion efficiency may be due to BKD. Affected fish often have pinpoint haemorrhages on the base of the pectoral fins and on the sides, with occasional popeye (*cf* VHS). If they are cut open, grey lesions ('granulomas') are evident in the kidney (Fig 59),

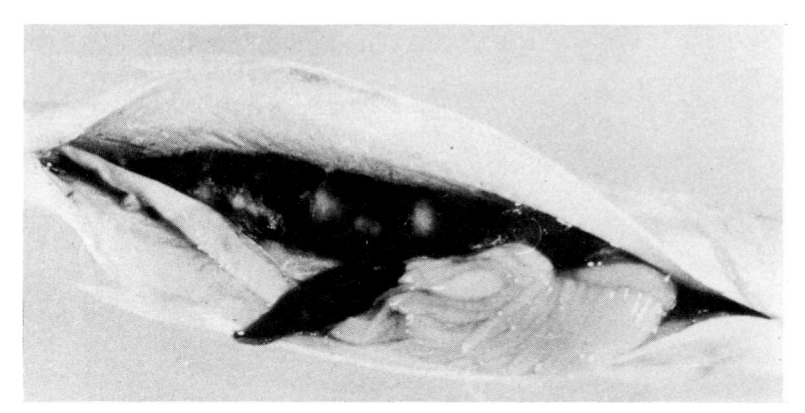

Fig 59   Bacterial Kidney Disease (BKD). The whitish lesions are seen in the kidney substance of this Atlantic salmon smolt infected with *Corynebacteria*.

and possibly also in the spleen and liver. Cavernous spaces may be found in muscle of affected fish especially Pacific salmon (Fig 60).

The disease is caused by bacteria which may infect the wild fish in a watershed, especially salmon. An adjacent fish farm can therefore become infected from wild fish, but the disease is more commonly introduced with infected fish brought-in from another farm. Treatment may be attempted by the use of sulphonamides in the feed over a long period (p 156).

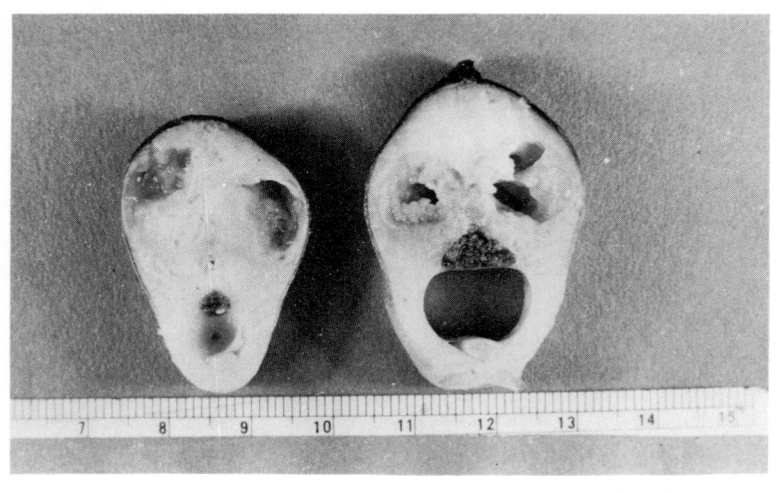

Fig 60   Severe Bacterial Kidney Disease (BKD). In Pacific salmon culture especially, there is frequently muscle involvement in BKD due to Corynebacterial infection. The cavernous lesions of the muscle are in addition to the small white granulomas in the kidney.

Photograph by courtesy of Prof R D Wolke.

(iv) Proliferative kidney disease (PKD)

This disease of rainbow trout is manifested by continuous low-grade losses of fish, which show pale gills and abdominal swelling. Losses increase rapidly if the fish are stressed or fed with antibiotics and/or sulphonamides. The cause is probably a protozoan parasite and diagnosis is by microscopic examination of the kidney, spleen and liver. Fingerlings are most frequently affected and when cut open show a greyish swelling of the kidney and spleen with fluid in the abdominal cavity (Fig 61).

2 Visceral granuloma/nephrocalcinosis

Visceral granuloma and nephrocalcinosis are probably different forms of the same disease condition of trout. This is a chronic disease characterized by losses occurring over a considerable period and any stress may increase the scale of losses. Visceral granuloma affects the stomach wall and nephrocalcinosis affects the kidney, while both seem to be associated with poor water quality (in particular high carbon dioxide levels) and possibly also dietary factors.

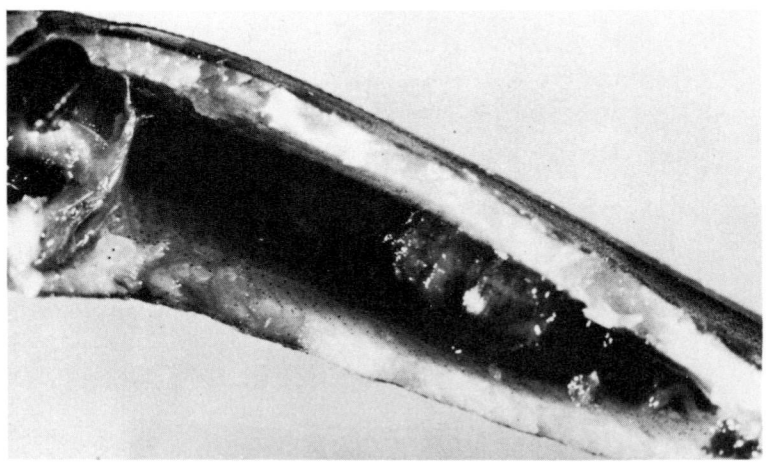

Fig 61   Proliferative Kidney Diseases (PKD). The grey shiny lesions in the swollen kidney require careful differentiation from Bacterial Kidney Disease (BKD) as both occur predominantly in soft waters.

Changes to the stomach involve small hard raised lumps on the stomach wall which spread to other abdominal organs. In the kidney the lesions occur as long grey strands of hardened tissue extending into the kidney from its surface and care should be taken to distinguish the condition from Bacterial Kidney Disease (BKD).

3 Bad-doers

The occurrence of fish which 'do badly' may usually be directly related to the husbandry conditions under which they are kept. Fish showing Fin Rot, and various external parasite infections, lose condition and frequently become secondarily invaded by bacteria and fungi (Fig 62). When such fish are cut open, they often show signs of internal

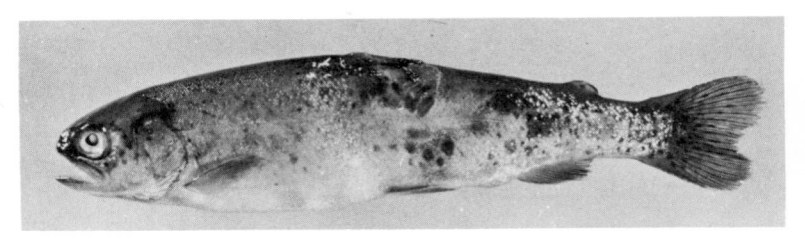

Fig 62   'Bad Doer'. Where stocking densities are high or water quality poor, ragged fins can be a sign that the fish are under stress, and bacterial or parasitic problems may soon follow.

parasitism. Roundworms, tapeworms and thorny-headed worms may be present in large numbers and protozoan parasites, particularly *Hexamita*, may also be evident in wet preparations of gut contents. These parasites multiply rapidly when the resistance of the host is poor and bad-doers will often provide a focus of infection for various agents.

The infection may then spread to healthy fish and although these may not show obvious wasting or permit the agents to multiply extensively, the conversion efficiency of the stock may fall significantly. This is particularly so with tapeworm infections which may be treated by the use of di-n-butyl tin oxide incorporated in the feed (p 156). Another consideration is that the presence of worm parasites can substantially reduce the market value and aesthetic appeal of fish, particularly if destined for human consumption.

Chapter IX Diseases of Marine Culture

As yet marine fish culture is in its infancy and it is probable that many diseases will be described as the industry develops. Already specific marine problems are becoming recognized, most of which look very similar to conditions occurring in fresh water. The main differences between marine and freshwater salmonid diseases derive from the particular salt requirements of certain infectious agents involved. The different types of husbandry also have an influence, especially the common use of trash fish diets and floating cages or nets in the case of marine systems.

A   ACUTE LOSSES

Fish kills under marine conditions are most often due to oxygen lack arising from poor water circulation. This can be a particular problem at periods of slack tide and is often exacerbated by the build-up of unused feed and metabolic wastes on the seabed. Once in the sea, salmonids have usually passed the stage of susceptibility to the dangerous virus diseases, although they may still carry the infection.

1 Vibriosis

The most severe disease problems of marine farms are caused by bacterial infections, notably with *Vibrio anguillarum*. The latter is the agent of vibriosis, to which many species of marine fish appear susceptible and can act as carriers. As with other acute bacterial diseases, salmonids usually show a short period of reduced appetite before losses start to occur. Dying fish are often dark in colour and when opened up they appear very haemorrhagic with swollen spleens and liquefied kidneys (Fig 63). Fish which survive longer often develop ulcers which erode the back muscles and the base of the fins. Vibriosis ulcers are rather deeper than those of furunculosis but the two diseases otherwise closely resemble each other.

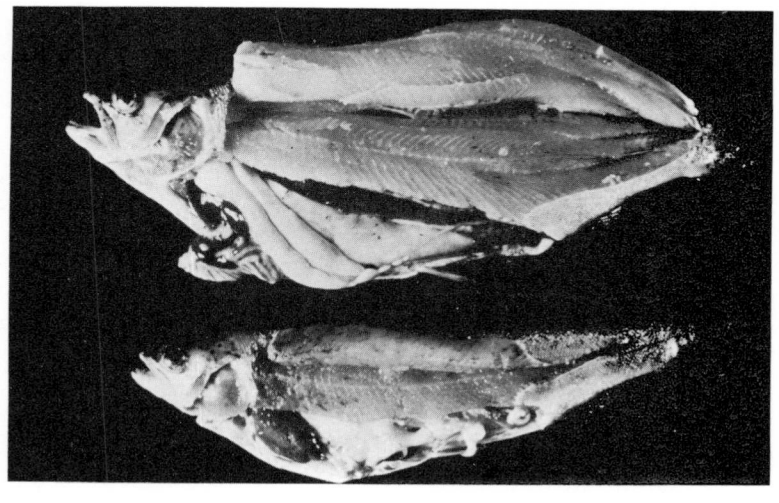

Fig 63   Vibriosis. The post-mortem picture in *Vibrio* infection is characterized by haemorrhages of the muscles and viscera and a swollen spleen.

Photograph by courtesy of Dr T Håstein.

The agent of vibriosis usually enters fish via skin wounds, and loss of scales after grading or transport etc predisposes to infection. Prompt treatment with antibiotics will usually save those fish which are still taking feed (p 156). Pasteurellosis is another acute infection due to a different bacterium. It has been reported from Norwegian waters and is virtually indistinguishable from vibriosis; it is treated in the same way.

2 Bacterial kidney disease (BKD)
Judging the correct time at which salmon smolts may be transferred from fresh to salt water is a skilled art. Recently this has been complicated still further by the sporadic occurrence of sudden mortalities in smolts soon after the transfer. Such fish are apparently ready to go to sea and have no external signs of disease. However on being opened up, small haemorrhages are visible on the surface of both liver and kidney, within which there are large white 'granulomatous' lesions (Fig 59). It seems that the kidneys of these fish have been undergoing severe damage over a long period due to Corynebacterial infection. Although often able to cope with the disease while in fresh water, the additional stress imposed by a saline environment apparently causes

119

kidney failure and rapid mortality. Treatment of these chronic infections is usually not practicable, and care should be taken to ensure that salmon eggs or parr come from an uninfected source.

B SKIN PROBLEMS

A number of common diseases of marine salmonids are manifested by skin problems. These are mostly of nuisance value rather than being the cause of severe economic loss. Provided prompt action is taken, they are unlikely to result in heavy mortalities.

1 Parasites

An example of this is the unsightly black spots which appear in the skin following infection with an intermediate stage (cercaria) of the fluke, *Cryptocotyle*. There is no treatment for this condition other than siting marine farms at a distance from beds of winkles as it is these molluscs which, together with sea birds, act as the intermediate hosts for the parasite. Severe 'Black-spot' infection will tend to reduce the value of salmon and massive fatal infections have been reported occasionally.

Sea Lice (*Lepeophtheirus*) can sometimes be an intractable problem. Although one or two lice are expected on wild salmon and may even enhance their market value, high density culture runs the risk of heavy infections with this prolific skin parasite. Affected fish may rub themselves on nets or cages, causing ulcers to form which allow the lice to eat deeper into the flesh. Such wounds sometimes appear, particularly on the head (Fig 64), and secondary infection can be rapidly fatal in certain cases. Treatment is not easy and organophosphorous compounds are most frequently used (p 152). Sea Lice require salt to survive and moving infected fish into fresh water will kill the parasite, although this is usually not a practical solution.

The occurrence of flashing among marine stock may be due to lice, but is more commonly a sign of monogenetic fluke infestation. Under unhygienic conditions or where there is overcrowding, parasites such as *Gyrodactylus* can multiply rapidly causing skin irritation with increased mucus secretion etc. The organism can be easily identified in skin scrapings and treatment is by formalin (p 150).

Fig 64   Sea lice. In Atlantic salmon culture the numbers of sea lice may increase so much that they spread over the body and cause severe skin damage, either by their feeding or by the fish consequently rubbing against the cage.

Photograph by courtesy of Dr T Håstein.

2 Myxobacteria

Most of the remaining skin problems are due in part to various species of myxobacteria. An exception is the virus of Salmon Pox which causes a similar condition to that of fish infected in fresh water, *ie* warts which can rub off leaving ulcerated areas which may become secondarily infected. Even in this case the secondary infection is likely to be with myxobacterial colonies and this may be sufficient to kill the fish.

Any form of damage to the skin is in fact likely to encourage myxobacterial infection in saltwater. Thus high stocking densities in metal cages can result in traumatic damage to the snout of salmonids and the resultant infection can extend to erode the entire head. The skin of fish which have started to mature takes on the characteristic changes associated with spawning. If such fish are not transferred to fresh water, the skin begins to slough, forming ulcers and myxobacteria rapidly takes over. At low water temperatures, certain myxobacteria cause thickening of the skin of the tail or fins without there necessarily being prior damage apparent. This 'Coldwater Disease' affects particularly

121

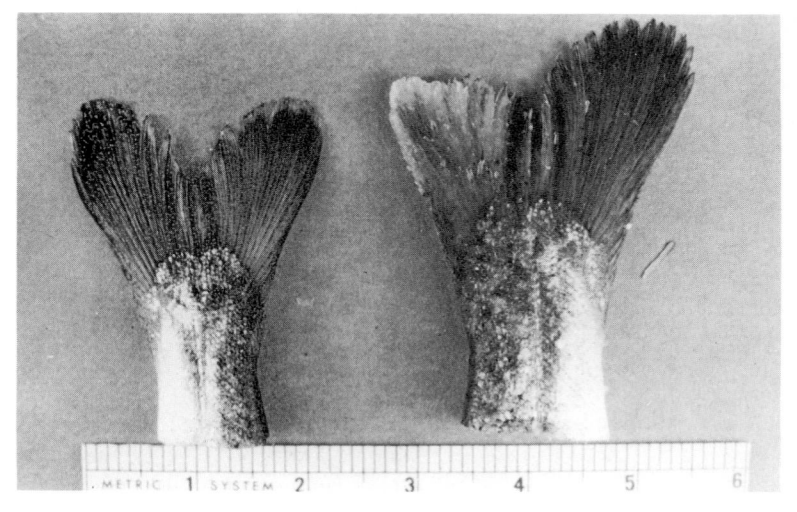

Fig 65   Cold water disease. In this picture, the larger of the two tails shows the beginning of cold water disease in a Pacific salmon. The affected part of the tail it thicker, greyish, and quickly becomes destroyed by myxobacteria.

Photograph by courtesy of Prof R D Wolke.

chinook and coho salmon which develop greyish-white extremities (Fig 65) and if the skin sloughs, subsequent invasion of the muscles will result in rapid death.

Where the initiating cause cannot be eliminated by better husbandry, transferring affected fish to fresh water will usually destroy the marine myxobacteria involved. This is a skilled process and unfortunately it is often difficult to achieve it without losing a varying proportion of the fish as well.

C FISH DIET INFECTIONS
The feeding of trash fish diets can result in a number of disease problems, including certain deficiency and toxic conditions described under Nutritional Diseases (p 124). It can also increase the spread of two infectious diseases, both of which are chronic wasting conditions which have been reported from marine fish farms.

1 Tuberculosis (TB) *Nocardia*
Tuberculosis and *Nocardia* are practically identical conditions which result in poor growth and the development of granular

122

and lumpy lesions throughout the body. Often the only outward signs of the disease are emaciation and a dark coloration, but at post-mortem examination the whitish lesions are easily visible particularly in the liver, spleen and kidney. The usual mode of infection is by a salmonid being fed on a diet of trash fish which have themselves been infected with TB/*Nocardia* organisms. If the disease is suspected, laboratory diagnosis is required. There is no satisfactory treatment and the disease can only be prevented with certainty by prior pasteurization of trash fish diets.

2 *Ichthyophonus*

Ichthyophonus is a similar disease to TB, although the causative agent is a fungus rather than a bacterium. When trash fish which are infected with *Ichthyophonus* are fed to salmonids, the fungus invades the gut and then progressively spreads throughout the internal organs. Affected fish fail to grow and, when opened at post-mortem examination, whitish nodules are evident, particularly in the heart, muscles, gut, liver and kidney (Fig 35). Diagnosis is made by squeezing one of the white lesions onto a slide; the characteristic branching structure of the fungus is evident under the microscope. Again treatment is not possible and prevention involves avoidance or pasteurization of infected trash fish.

Chapter X Nutritional Diseases

Although fry may have difficulty in getting onto feed, especially in the case of Atlantic salmon (p 87), subsequent undernourishment is usually due to poor management which may be complicated by disease problems. With the increased use of scientifically formulated diets, diseases due to *malnutrition*, *ie* incorrect dietary composition, have become increasingly rare. Occasionally, however, they may still occur, particularly if an inexperienced fish-farmer attempts to prepare his own diets. Nevertheless, in general the composition of the diet should be the last line of enquiry in any disease investigation, after prior consideration of more likely causes.

With the exception of certain problems arising from moist trash fish diets (notably Botulism/Bankruptcy disease: p 102) nutritional diseases tend to be chronic conditions which appear over an extended period of time. The usual signs comprise low-level mortalities, wasting, reduced conversion efficiency and internal changes, particularly in the liver, kidney and skeleton (Fig 66). Because of this often ill-defined picture of poor health and their comparative rarity, nutritional diseases will be divided up according to the nature of the dietary component involved, rather than the outward appearance of the fish. Four categories of nutritional diseases will be considered; the first three arise from feeding levels of (A) Vitamins, (B) Minerals and trace elements, and (C) Fats — which are outside the required prosperity range for salmonids. The fourth category (D) comprises miscellaneous conditions which are thought to have a nutritional origin including those arising from the presence of contaminants in the diet.

A   VITAMIN DISEASES

Vitamins are usually divided into those which are soluble in

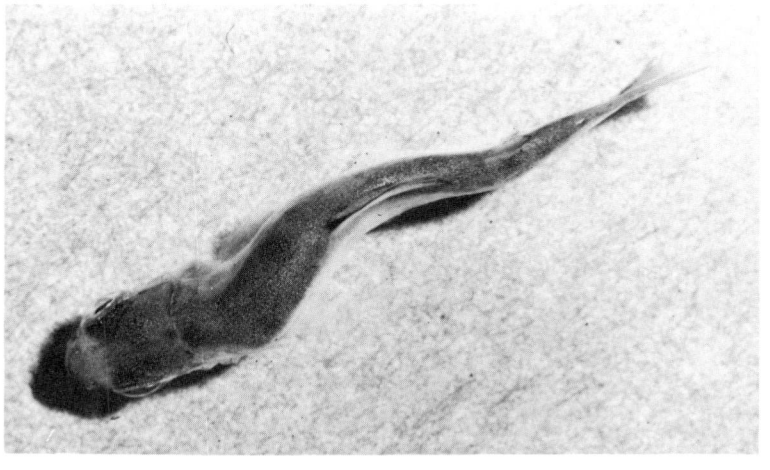

Fig 66   Skeletal Malformation. This fish was on an experimental diet deficient in vitamin D, and the spine is consequently twisted.

water (the B group) and those which are soluble in fat (all the rest). Deficiencies of most vitamins in each class can cause disease in salmonids but in practice vitamin B deficiencies are commonest.

1 Fat soluble vitamin deficiencies
Deficiencies of Vitamins A, D, E and K can probably all cause diseases of salmonids, with poor growth and anaemia being common symptoms. Vitamin E is required for fat digestion and there may be insufficient of this vitamin to deal with diets having a high fat content (see under 'Fats'). The main distinguishing features of deficiencies of Vitamins A, D (and C), and K are: blindness, bone malformations, and impaired blood coagulation respectively.

2 Water soluble vitamin deficiencies
(i) Thiamine (B_1) deficiency

This deficiency most commonly arises due to the use of certain trash fish diets, *eg* herring, which contains an enzyme (thiaminase) which destroys thiamine. This results in brain degeneration with consequent loss of balance, nervous convulsions, blindness etc. In countries where trash fish feeding is commonly practised, it is usual to incorporate an additive into the diet containing high levels of thiamine in order to prevent the deficiency.

(ii) Riboflavin (B$_2$) Deficiency
Eye changes are characteristic of this condition, notably lens opacity (cataract) and haemorrhages into the eye. Affected fish are usually dark in colour.

(iii) Pantothenic acid deficiency
Deficiency of this vitamin causes an uncommon but characteristic gill disease in fast growing salmonid fry. These show loss of appetite and gasping, due to the gill lamellae thickening and then becoming fused to each other. This nutritional gill disease can be distinguished from commoner gill problems, *eg* Bacterial gill disease, by the microscopical appearance of the fused lamellae.

(iv) Other B group vitamin deficiencies
Pyridoxine deficiency can cause similar nervous signs to those of thiamine (B$_1$) deficiency with the occurrence of convulsive fits. Niacin deficiency may cause uncoordinated muscle movements and swollen gills. Biotin deficiency may affect the skin of salmonids and render it more liable to parasitic infections. These and other deficiency syndromes (*eg* Vitamin C) are usually characterized by reduced appetite and growth and a tendency to anaemia.

B   MINERAL AND TRACE ELEMENT DISEASES
A number of elements are considered essential for salmonids including: calcium, chlorine, cobalt, copper, iodine, iron, magnesium, manganese, phosphorus, potassium, selenium, sodium, sulphur and zinc. Deficiency of these elements is rarely a problem, although iodine deficiency used to cause swelling of the thyroid gland ('goitre') prior to the use of fish meal in compounded diets. The requirement for certain of these elements is extremely small and the presence of such 'trace elements' in larger amounts will often provoke disease. This can be a particular problem with heavy metals such as iron, copper and zinc, which may enter a water supply from natural rock deposits, metal pipes, or with industrial effluents. Iron salts can form a precipitate on fish gills or on the surface of eggs causing asphyxiation of the embryo.

Copper and zinc toxicity may be manifested by respiratory difficulties with pale gills becoming coated with mucus. The toxicity of these heavy metals is often markedly increased in soft water.

C   FAT DISEASES

Salmonids have specific requirements for at least one fatty acid but deficiencies are unlikely to occur under farm conditions (there are similarly requirements for certain aminoacids which are usually satisfied by diets of fish protein).

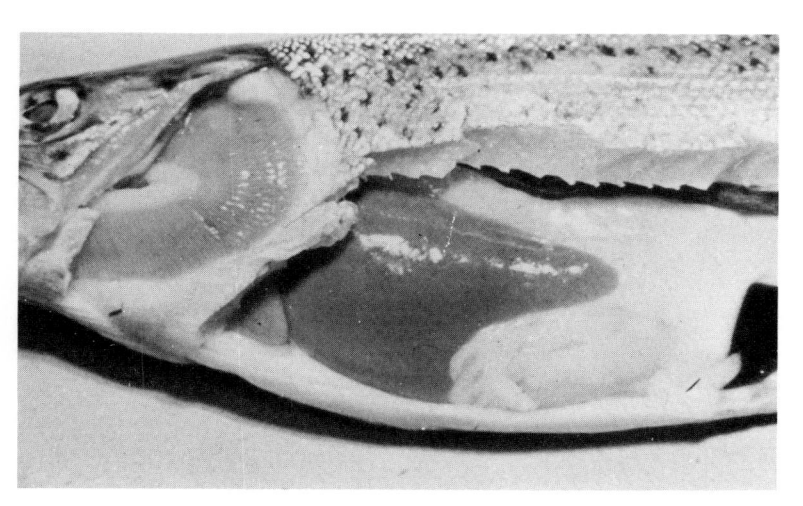

Fig 67   Fatty Liver. The liver is bronze in colour and has rounded edges. There is marked anaemia and much fat around the viscera.
Photograph by courtesy of Dr T Håstein.

Lipoid liver degeneration due to fatty infiltration of the liver is a common finding in farmed salmonids. This results from the digestive system being overloaded by feeding high levels of unsuitable ('unsaturated') fat, which may be derived from fish (especially herring), slaughterhouse offals, or even silkworm pupae. In mild cases, the typically bronze-coloured liver may only be discovered at gutting (Fig 67). However, in more severe cases the liver swells up, haemorrhages can occur in the viscera, and the gills may appear pale. Such fish are weak, anaemic, and may die when handled.

127

D MISCELLANEOUS NUTRITIONAL DISEASES

1 Aflatoxins

The presence of large tumours of the liver, particularly in rainbow trout, is usually indicative of aflatoxin poisoning. When ground nuts and cottonseed are stored, they sometimes become mouldy, and aflatoxins are poisons produced by these moulds. Some months after trout are fed even minute quantities of mouldy oil seeds, liver tumours ('hepatomas') appear and these can spread rapidly through the body and cause large losses. Cottonseed can also cause disease more directly due to the presence of a toxic pigment causing inappetance and fatty deposits in the liver and kidney.

2 Botulism

Botulism is a disease of many animals including fish and also humans in which it is nearly always rapidly fatal. It arises due to the ingestion of the toxin produced by a bacterium, *Clostridium botulinum*. This organism is usually in harmless spore form, but under certain conditions of warmth and oxygen lack, may start to produce the lethal *botulinum* toxin.

If wet trash fish feed is allowed to go rotten, it will sometimes form this toxin and cause botulism in salmonids to which it is fed. Affected fish suddenly go off their feed and develop nervous signs, sinking to the bottom of the pond apparently lifeless and then twitching back to the surface again (Bankruptcy disease p 102).

The spores of the *botulinum* organism occur commonly in soil and mud and are therefore common inhabitants of the intestines of healthy salmonids under many farming conditions. When operating a smoking kiln for processing fish, care must be taken to ensure that fish are hygienically gutted and that the conditions under which toxin formation can take place are avoided. Otherwise there is a remote possibility that fatal human botulism can occur from eating the contaminated product, particularly if it has not been pre-cooked.

Chapter XI Fish Kills

If a sudden mass-mortality occurs over a period of hours (or less) among fish which have been behaving and feeding normally, then the situation is designated a 'Fish-kill'. Such an event cannot be due to infectious disease and may involve the possibility of litigation. Therefore, it is vital to act swiftly, not only for the purpose of saving as many fish as possible.

Fish kills can be caused in a variety of ways, but the commonest is lack of oxygen. This often occurs under conditions of high temperature and low water flows when the fish are fed heavily. In ponds with much algal growth, oxygen deficiency may build up in the early hours of the morning, particularly if there is no wind to mix the various water layers (this is because plants use up oxygen during the hours of darkness). In such cases the kill may not be total and fish may be seen gasping in obvious distress. Blocked filters or pump breakdowns usually precipitate heavy fish kills unless noticed immediately, and the dead fish may show haemorrhages in the skin and within the gut cavity.

Many forms of pollution kill fish by lack of oxygen. Thus most agricultural effluents, *eg* silage liquor, decrease the oxygen-carrying capacity of the water until there is insufficient oxygen available for fish to survive. Whenever pumps are closed down for maintenance, care should be taken to ensure that the consequent rotting of plants and organisms within the pipelines does not result in lethal pollution when the system is put into operation once again.

Cyanide kills by preventing fish from utilizing oxygen, and poachers frequently use various preparations of cyanide. Such fish will appear to have died quietly without any obvious signs, although they may possess a characteristic 'burnt almonds' smell. Many industrial effluents are toxic to fish, particularly heavy metals and hydrocarbons. Lead, copper, iron, zinc, and molybdenum have all been implicated in fish kills. Great care should always be taken when handling disinfectants on fish farms. Iodophors, which are so useful for killing fish viruses must not be allowed to come into contact with live fish; if they enter a fish pond accidentally, the fish will sometimes literally leap out of the water. Insecticides and weedkillers are often a problem and most organochloride and organophosphorous compounds are highly toxic. In the case of Dieldrin poisoning, the gills may appear yellow in colour. Alkaloids from rotting leaves occasionally result in fish mortalities and this may occur under spate conditions associated with low pH due to mineral acids entering a water supply deficient in buffering salts (p 95). Algal toxins have also been reported as killing salmonids in warm weather, although this may be due in part to removal of oxygen by the algal blooms at night-time. Finally, it should be born in mind that most chemicals added to the water for treating fish diseases are themselves toxic to fish at all concentrations except very low ones.

On discovering a fish kill, it is advisable to call the police immediately unless the cause is obviously the farm's own fault (*eg* a blocked filter). The manner of dying and the symptoms shown should be written down and the extent of the kill throughout the farm should be noted. Think before you act! If an affected pond drains into a stocked outlet channel, it may be preferable to shut it off rather than increase the flow rate and kill the fish in the channel as well. Nevertheless the prompt use of aerators, auxiliary pumps etc, and transferring survivors to clean water, can often reduce losses considerably.

Water samples should be placed in clean (lead-free) bottles and sealed in the presence of two witnesses. Newly dead fish should be placed in deep freeze. Dying fish should be killed, and small cubes of the organs (especially liver, kidney, gut, skin, and gills) should be placed in a pickling liquid — 1 : 10 solution of 40% formalin, or formal saline, or 'Bouin's fluid'. If cyanide poisoning is suspected, heads of affected fish should be forwarded to the appropriate laboratory. Photographs may be a useful aid should litigation ensue, and a comprehensive account of the incident should be recorded and forwarded to the appropriate bodies if any further action is envisaged.

Chapter XII
Diseases of Wild Fish and Broodstock

Diseases of wild fish have an intrinsic interest for the angler or netsman, because they can affect the abundance and aesthetic appeal of his quarry. They are also extremely significant to the fish farmer since wild fish can act as carriers for a number of the major disease agents. In addition many fish farms rely on the capture of mature wild fish to provide the eggs and milt for hatchery operations. Brood fish on the farm are usually kept in somewhat similar conditions to those in the wild, being less densely stocked than growers. They share many disease problems with wild fish and these will be considered together in this chapter.

As in the farm situation, very severe losses are invariably due to non-infectious causes, and are considered under 'Fish Kills' (p 129). In heavily stocked fisheries with abundant aquatic vegetation, fish kills due to oxygen lack are a not uncommon occurrence. Pollution is always a danger and in the case of valuable adult fish, malicious use of substances such as cyanide, carbide or dynamite must be considered.

Leaving aside fish kills, diseases of wild fish and broodstock can be broadly divided into three groups: acute infectious diseases; diseases recognized mainly by skin lesions; and a miscellaneous group recognized incidentally at post-mortem. Except where relevant to management of broodstock, details of therapy are omitted since this is not generally feasible for wild fish. For those diseases shared by wild and farmed fish, such information is available elsewhere in the text.

A ACUTE INFECTIOUS DISEASES
Acute infections occurring among broodstock or in the wild are generally due to bacteria. Broodstock show a short period

131

of inappetance before the onset of quite heavy losses, which is usually the first sign to the angler of any disease problem. Under certain circumstances, acute infections will also result in the appearance of haemorrhagic ulcers on the outside of the fish, but these will be described in the next section (p 134).

If dead or dying fish with no external signs are opened up acute infections can be recognized by a variety of internal changes, the commonest of which is the presence of haemorrhages on the internal organs. During high water temperatures, this is the typical picture shown by young salmonids suffering from acute furunculosis due to *Aeromonas salmonicida* infection.

If small white lesions are also visible scattered throughout the spleen, kidney, and liver, then the causative organisms may be *Corynebacteria*, which can be responsible for sudden losses in some areas. The species most severely affected is the Atlantic salmon and the condition is so frequent in certain years in the Scottish river Dee that it is referred to as Dee disease. Unlike furunculosis, Dee disease can also occur at very low temperatures (*ca* 4°C). In this case, diseased fish show a white tenacious membrane stretched over the liver, kidney, and spleen, instead of the combination of white spots and haemorrhage shown at high temperatures.

The bacteria which cause these infections often survive between outbreaks of disease within the tissues of carrier fish. These fish can release them into the water to continue the infection while remaining apparently healthy. Because of this danger, eggs from rivers with a high incidence of such diseases should not be taken for stocking fish hatcheries.

B DISEASES CHARACTERIZED BY SKIN LESIONS

A variety of diseases of wild fish and broodstock are manifested by obvious skin abnormalities. These may be conveniently classified into those diseases associated with sexual maturity, and others, and they will be discussed accordingly in this section. In general, salmonids showing the pale skin patches associated with fungus infection may be assumed to be suffering from one of the diseases associated with sexual maturity.

1 Diseases associated with sexual maturity

The hormones which cause the gonads to develop within

salmonids bring about a variety of additional effects. Thus in the case of Pacific salmon they result in the virtual breakdown of all bodily systems and death ensues soon after spawning. In most salmonids the stomach and intestine change markedly at the onset of sexual maturity and become incapable of digestion. The skin also changes in various ways depending on the species. It actually becomes thicker in male fish and the mucus alters to a more viscous consistency.

Salmonid skin appears more prone to infection while undergoing these changes around spawning time. Physical damage to the skin is also more liable to occur while fish are migrating to their spawning redds and fighting among broodstock males often results in injuries. Such wounds heal more slowly on account of the low water temperature. In addition there may be a greater number of fungal spores present in rivers during this season. Certainly many fish become severely infected with fungi, especially *Saprolegnia*. Creamy-coloured patches of fungus appear on any part of the skin and these often kill the fish outright (Fig 68). They may follow skin trauma, due to seal damage, stab wounds caused by birds, netting marks etc, but can also result from ulcers caused by disease. If lightly affected fish regain the sea, the fungus usually disappears, although contraction of the resulting scar can sometimes cause permanent deformity.

Fig 68   Fungus infection. The *Saprolegnia* covers most of the body in this spawning brown trout.

Fish which are severely affected with fungus should be removed from the river, killed, and examined, before being buried, preferably in a lime pit. The presence of ulcers on the head, or haemorrhages inside the body, should suggest the possibility of two specific diseases which are discussed in more detail.

(i) Autumn aeromonad disease

This is a condition which mainly affects adult brown trout during the spawning season. Such fish show patches of skin fungus due to *Saprolegnia* and sometimes the skin overlying the gut cavity may show severe inflammation (Fig 69). The main feature of the disease is the state of the internal organs which are usually very haemorrhagic. The kidney is often completely liquefied so that when incised, it flows out of its capsule.

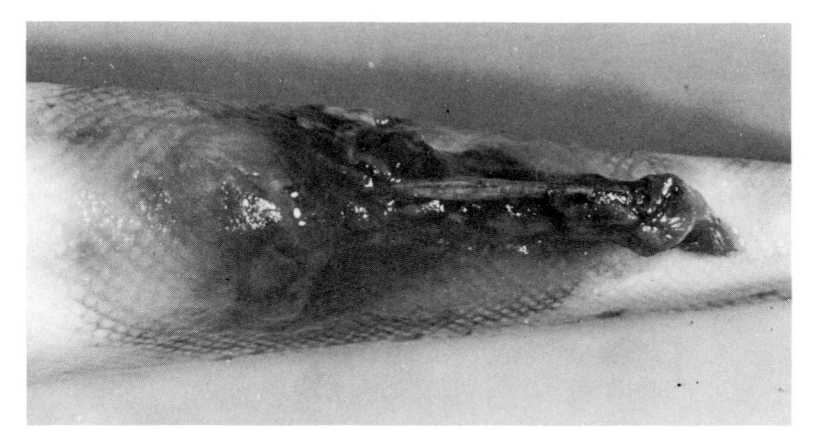

Fig 69   Autumn Aeromonad disease. The lesions of this disease are bright red in colour and often found near the vent. An added complication in this fish is the prolapse of the anal and urogenital area.

The disease is associated with generalized bacterial infection usually with *Aeromonas hydrophila* or related bacteria, which can be isolated from all organs in the laboratory. However, the primary cause would appear to be the stresses associated with spawning. Thus immature fish, or adults which are not spawning, may carry the bacteria responsible for the disease, but are themselves completely unaffected.

(ii) Ulcerative dermal necrosis (UDN)

This is a disease of unknown cause which was originally described as affecting Atlantic salmon and sea trout as they came into fresh water. UDN is confined to adult fish and has at present only been described from Ireland, Britain and France.

In migratory salmonids the disease characteristically occurs during the colder months of the year. It usually starts as the fish enter fresh water for their spawning run and the first signs are very small greyish lesions on the side of the opercula, above the eyes or on the snout (Fig 70). These either heal or spread to involve a greater area of the head. They then ulcerate to produce a reddish wound, which becomes infected by bacteria or fungus from the surface of the fish or the water. The fungus spreads from the initial site of infection to the rest of the weakened fish, which thus becomes indistinguishable from any other fish with a severe fungus infection.

There is very little information available on the disease in brown and rainbow trout. Certainly a disease similar to classical UDN of salmon occurs in maturing fish in certain fish farms and rivers during autumn. The lesions are confined to the head and are not at first affected by fungus. In the absence of any diagnostic test only tentative diagnosis is possible. This is usually based on the findings in the early stages of uninfected head lesions in adult fish.

There is no evidence that lightly affected fish cannot spawn successfully or that their offspring are either more or less susceptible to the disease. However, in view of the probable infectious nature of UDN, it would seem sensible to take hygienic precautions with fishing tackle and clothing if moving from an infected to an uninfected water, and to avoid the introduction of eggs from an infected river to a previously clean hatchery. If lightly affected fish are taken for stripping, the disease can usually be cured by treatment with malachite green, since the internal organs are not affected until secondary infection has progressed.

2 Diseases unassociated with sexual maturity

Several diseases which are sometimes seen among wild salmonids are not specifically linked to sexual maturity and these include skin tumours and certain acute infections characterized by skin ulcers.

The presence of skin lesions on dead and dying fish without visible signs of fungus infection is usually evidence of acute bacterial infections. Grey head lesions, which may superficially resemble UDN ulcers, are usually caused by *Flexibacter columnaris*, if occurring at temperatures exceeding 20° C. This 'Columnaris' disease is mainly found in wild Pacific salmon and is rapidly fatal over 25° C. Microscopical examination of a scraping from ulcers of affected fish demonstrates the characteristic columns of bacteria and permits differentiation from UDN.

A more common skin manifestation of acute bacterial disease is the appearance of furuncles and/or deep haemorrhagic ulcers. Furunculosis, due to *Aeromonas salmonicida* infection, is usually evidenced in older fish by the classical sign of furuncles developing over the sides and back (Fig 11d — frontispiece). These sometimes burst and release haemorrhagic and highly infectious fluid. *Vibrio anguillarum* infection is a major cause of losses among salmonids returning from the sea into estuarine conditions. Vibriosis results in the formation of deep haemorrhagic abscesses within the muscles, with concurrent darkening or ulceration of the overlying skin. When fish affected with either furunculosis or vibriosis are opened up, haemorrhages of the internal organs are usually found, sometimes accompanied by swelling of the spleen and liquefaction of the kidney. Although affected broodstock may sometimes be saved by antibiotic and sulphonamide treatment, affected wild stock are best killed and buried, and every practical precaution taken to limit the spread of these contagious diseases.

Tumours are not infrequently encountered among wild fish including both benign and malignant tumours. A malignant tumour ('cancer') grows rapidly and spreads throughout the body, whereas a benign tumour merely increases in size slowly at its original site. Internal tumours sometimes occur, particularly arising from blood-forming tissues. These are usually seen only on gutting the fish, except in the case of tumours of the thymus gland beneath the gills. Several such tumours have been reported and may be recognized by the swollen-head appearance of affected fish resulting from pressure on the opercula (Fig 71). Skin tumours usually comprise whitish coloured lumps or raised, bleeding ulcers, especially if malignant (Fig 72). A fairly

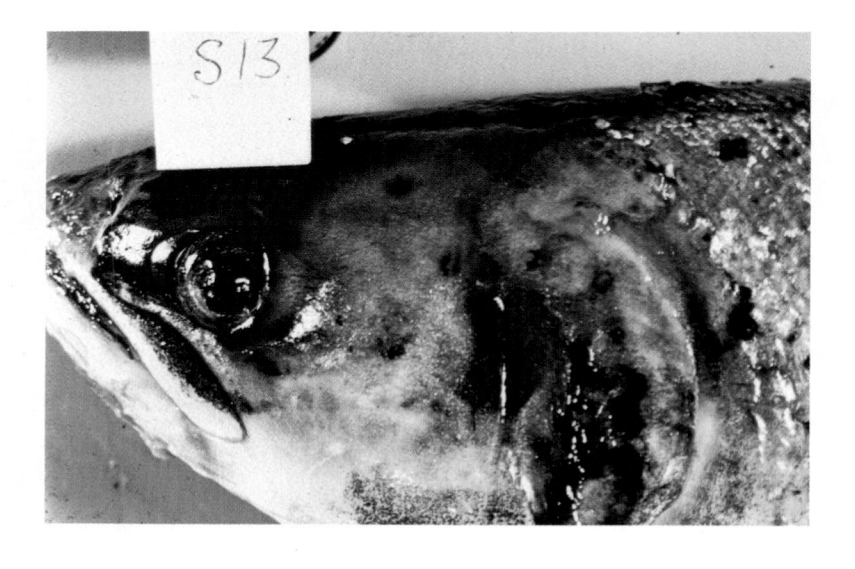

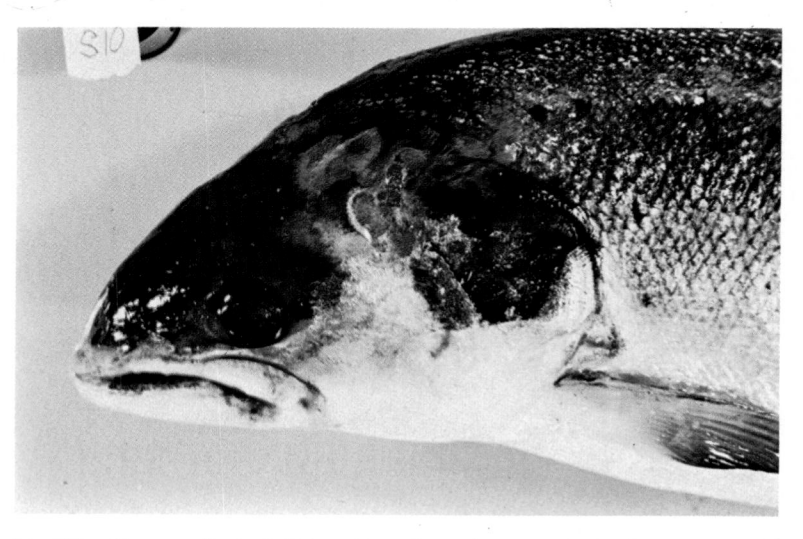

Fig 70 Uncomplicated Ulcerative dermal necrosis in Salmonids. (a)
The earliest stage of UDN, seen in Atlantic salmon as they enter fresh
water. The very small ulcer with the greyish halo around it may heal or
develop to the second stage where it becomes infected by water borne
bacteria or *Saprolegnia* fungus. (b) A later stage in the early UDN
lesions on fresh run Atlantic salmon. There are several ulcers on the side
of the head and usually such lesions are symmetrically placed on either

side. (c) A healing UDN lesion. This fish was kept in fresh water with added malachite green fungistat. This prevented the secondary infection and the picture shows the whitish scar tissue completing the cover of the raw ulcer. (d) Severe UDN in a large sea trout. This fish had been in the river for some time, but although the lesion was long standing, it had not become secondarily infected.

Fig 71   Thymic tumour in a rainbow trout. This tumour appears as a large pink swelling at the top of the gill cavity, and consists of altered tissue from the thymus gland.

Photograph by courtesy of Mr J F McArdle.

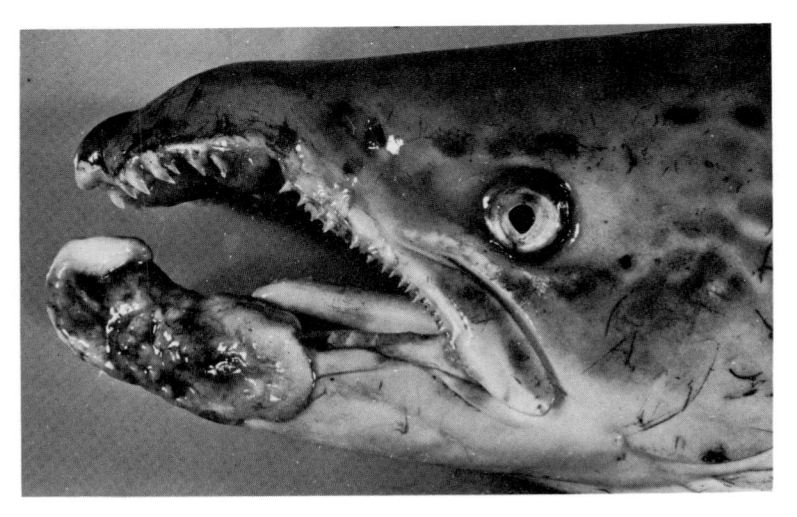

Fig 72   Skin cancer in an Atlantic salmon. This malignant tumour is affecting both the upper and lower jaw.

common benign tumour of salmon skin is probably caused by a virus. This is known as 'Salmon Pox' and results in warty growths on the fins and body. Salmon pox usually clears up eventually, but if warts become rubbed off the fish, the resulting ulcers are readily infected by fungi or bacteria.

In certain salmon rivers it has been known for a long time that fish can develop an area of grey, rough skin right on top of the head (Fig 52). It appears that this is simply due to sunburn and on occasion these 'Bald Spots' can become inflamed, ulcerated and secondarily infected. The same condition has been reported from fish farms in brook and rainbow trout, especially if shallow raceways are used.

C DISEASES DISCOVERED AT POST-MORTEM
There are a number of parasitic conditions which affect wild salmonids without usually causing frank disease. These are often discovered incidentally when the fish is captured, particularly when cleaned prior to cooking. Most of these parasites are incapable of developing and causing disease in man, even if eaten uncooked. However, they are often unsightly and reduce the aesthetic appeal of the catch.

1 External parasites

(i) Eyes
Blindness due to Eye Fluke infestation can be a severe problem in certain lakes where there are a large number of infected snails present.

(ii) Gills
Monogenetic flukes may be just visible on the gills of salmonids held in heavily stocked fisheries. After adult salmon have returned to fresh water they can also develop heavy infections with Gill Maggots. Since these maggots can survive on kelts returning to the sea, freshly-run repeat spawners may be readily recognized by the very large numbers of maggots sometimes present (Fig 73). Gill maggots are not normally considered harmful to salmon, but secondary fungal infection of damaged gills may cause occasional losses among kelts.

(iii) Skin
Skin infections with small *protozoa* and flukes can cause irritation and excess mucus secretion when the causative

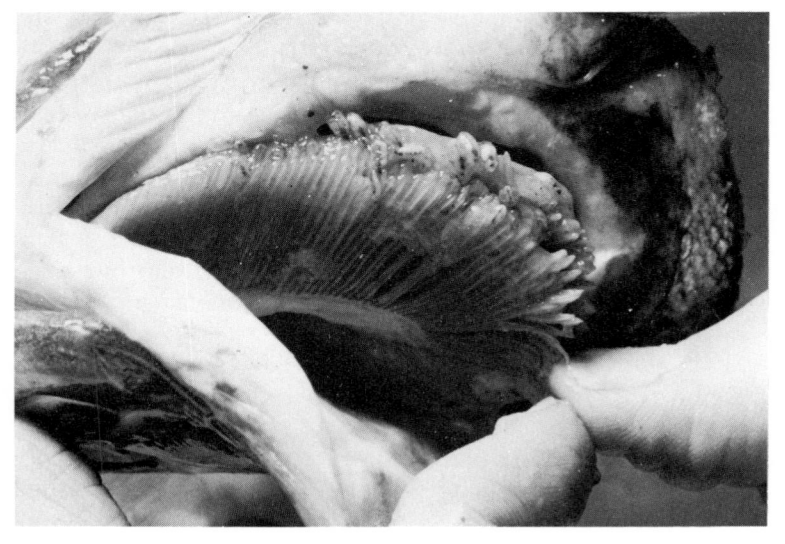

Fig 73   Parasitized Gills. The gills of this Atlantic salmon are heavily infected with gill maggots (see Fig 23), which results in a coat of thick mucus and small haemorrhages.

organism is often invisible to the naked eye. White Spot (Ich) can be a considerable problem in young fish under conditions of high water temperature. This is especially so when the water is shared by a population of coarse fish and there is a low flow-rate.

Of the larger crustacean parasites, both 'Fish Lice' and 'Sea Lice' are found on salmonids. The Fish Louse is found only in warmer waters and is of little significance except when heavy infestations provide sites for secondary infection. The presence of Sea Lice on salmon is welcome evidence of freshly-run fish and they are usually sited near the vent or in the tail region (see Fig 22).

2 Internal parasites

The only salmonid parasite which is very dangerous to man is a small white coiled worm occasionally seen on the surface of the liver, or other internal organs, of salmon and sea trout. These *Anisakis* worms are parasites of marine fish, and salmon can become infected by eating krill. *Anisakis* can cause severe intestinal damage to humans if swallowed live, but this is unlikely to happen unless raw fish is eaten.

141

Another parasite which is pathogenic to man is the tapeworm, *Diphyllobothrium latum*. This is one of a family of tapeworms which use various fish as host for one of their intermediate stages, and usually form an adult tapeworm in the gut of fish-eating birds. In heavy infections, the larval 'pleurocercoids' can cause mortality of fish as they migrate through the body tissues to the abdominal cavity or muscles. If infected fish are eaten uncooked, *eg* as lightly salted fish, the adult tapeworm can survive within the human intestine, where it has been known to cause 'Pernicious Anaemia', due to induced Vitamin B_{12} deficiency.

Much more common are the red coiled filariid or spilurid worms which move across the body surface of heavily infected fish when they are cut open. Although of no danger to man, these worms are particularly unattractive. Salmonids usually respond to their presence by laying down a large fluid-filled cyst within the abdominal cavity. This usually represents an intermediate larval stage of the parasite, whose adult life is spent in the stomach of fish-eating birds.

Sometimes when the angler cuts into the flesh of apparently healthy salmon or sea trout, certain areas of muscle may appear to have been replaced by a yellow creamy fluid. This is the condition of 'Milky Flesh' disease, due to a protozoan parasite, *Henneguya*, and severely affected fish are useless for the table.

When gutting salmon and trout, certain other parasites may be seen, particularly if the gut is accidentally incised. Thus if the swimbladder appears to be stuffed with cotton-wool, this is probably due to large numbers of *Cystidicola* worms, which are of little significance. More harmful to fish are certain Thorny-headed worms (*Acanthocephalus*) present in wild salmonids in most areas. They become attached to the intestinal wall (Fig 74) and in severe infections can cause obvious gut haemorrhage and loss of weight, increasing the risk of secondary infections. Care should be taken when introducing freshwater shrimps in order to improve a fishery as these carry an intermediate stage of the worm. Affected broodstock can be treated by medication with di-n-butyl tin oxide incorporated in the feed. The same drug is also of some value in treating tapeworm infestations among broodstock (p 156). Tape-worms are frequently also seen within the intestines of wild salmonids, notably *Eubothrium*, which may be present in

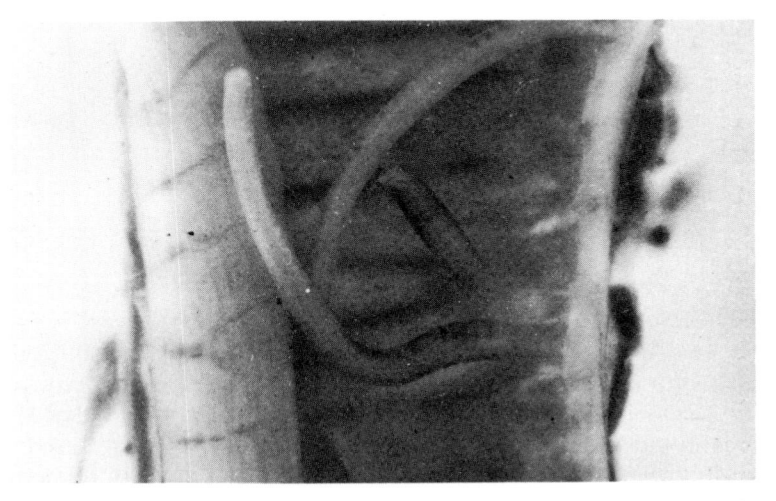

Fig 74   *Acanthocephalus* infection. The parasites are attached to the lining of the gut by the thorny proboscis at the head. The intestine is reddened and the gut mucus may be haemorrhagic.

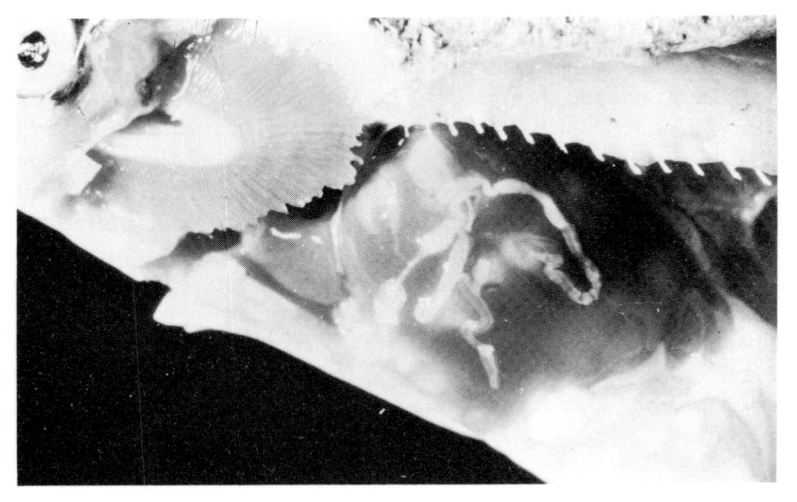

Fig 75   *Triaenophorus* infection. The intermediate stage of the *Triaenophorus* tapeworm is encysted in the liver of this rainbow trout.
Photograph by courtesy of Dr T Håstein.

large numbers without causing apparent harm to the fish or reducing its value for the table. In waters which contain large numbers of pike, pleurocercoid stages of *Triaenophorus* tapeworms may be found in every salmonid (Fig 75), and occasionally heavy infections result in thin and wasted fish.

Chapter XIII
Prevention and Treatment of Disease

1 Disease prevention

It has been emphasized that careful attention to good husbandry and fish management are essential in the control of disease. The use of bore-hole water, compounded diets, gravel filters on hatchery water supply etc, will greatly reduce the likelihood of many diseases, particularly parasitic infections. Others, notably viral diseases must be prevented from entering the farm lest they become established. Such diseases commonly enter a farm along with eggs or live fish. They can also enter via the water supply, wild fish, birds and their droppings, fish food, and on the hands and especially the boots of farm personnel and lorry drivers.

Salmonid eggs should only be ordered from a farm which has been certified by a competent laboratory as being free of the important virus diseases. Before arrival at their destination, they should be disinfected, transferred into a clean utensil and the original packaging burnt. An iodophor disinfectant should be used, such as Wescodyne, at a concentration of 50-100 ppm, into which the eggs should be dipped for 10 minutes. Such iodophors are very acidic and must thus be neutralized with a suitable buffer (*eg* sodium bicarbonate) to prevent harming the eggs at disinfection. Live fish should never be introduced from another source, unless absolutely necessary. In this case, they should be placed on arrival at the farm in special quarantine ponds, where they must be held completely separated from other fish for at least a month.

Care should be taken to ensure not only that disease does not enter the farm, but also that if a disease appears in one pond, cross-infection to other ponds will not necessarily follow. It is preferable to permit only the supervisor to enter the hatchery building and he should be required to walk through a foot bath of disinfectant solution on entry. If possible, there should be a different dip-net provided for, and

144

restricted to, each pond. Transfer of fish from one pond to another should be kept to the minimum necessary. Any dead fish should be buried in a lime pit away from the ponds, and birds should be discouraged by predator netting, scarers, shooting etc. For purposes of hygiene, the iodophor disinfectants are preferable because of their virucidal activity. They are extremely toxic to fish and will precipitate a fish kill if they enter the water supply. The presence of any organic matter markedly reduces the effectiveness of iodophors and equipment should be cleaned, *eg* with a pressure hose, before disinfection.

Earth ponds should be drained completely and allowed to remain dry for a month each year. Sunlight has a marked disinfectant action and this is therefore best done in the summer. If a stronger action is required *eg* following an outbreak of Whirling disease, quicklime (calcium oxide) may be spread over the bottom of the pond at an application rate of 1 lb/sq yd. Following an outbreak of virus disease, it may be desirable to kill out the entire farm, disinfect and then restock. In this case, earth ponds should be drained before spraying with a mixed solution[1] of Teepol and Caustic Soda. The mixture comprises one part of Teepol to 25 parts of 0.1 N. sodium hydroxide and it is sprayed at a rate of half gallon/sq yd. If fabricated systems such as fibreglass are being cleared of virus infection, then iodophor solutions are best used after scrubbing (*eg* 1% Vanodine FAM). In this situation it should always be borne in mind that if wild fish in the watershed have contracted the infection, they are likely to remain carriers and may subsequently act as a source of reinfection.

2 Record-keeping

This is an appropriate stage in the text to emphasize the crucial importance of maintaining good records. Initial site evaluation should provide details of seasonal changes in physical and chemical factors of the water supply, *eg* drought flow rate, or hardness. However, day-to-day monitoring of various factors permits more efficient use of growing facilities under conditions which are often changing rapidly. These factors may be summarized as follows:

   (i) Water flow
  (ii) Fish weight (unit and total weights per pond)
 (iii) Water temperature

(iv) Water chemistry — oxygen, pH, ammonia, salinity.
(v) Weight of feed used
(vi) Losses
(vii) Drugs used and details of treatment

Water flow is most commonly measured simply by determining the time taken to fill a container (or pond) of known volume. Accurate knowledge of the usable volume of pond space available, together with the flow rate data should allow estimation of the stocking rates to be used. Water temperature data is also required and permits estimation of feed requirements for a certain stock of given unit weight. Particularly under very intensive conditions at high water temperatures, monitoring of water chemistry factors such as dissolved oxygen and total ammonia helps to show when danger levels are being approached. pH recordings will allow calculation of free ammonia present from the value of total ammonia, and under marine conditions a salinometer will show any fluctuations in salt concentration. Losses should be counted daily and, when incorporated into the feed consumption and conversion efficiency calculations for a given pond, often give valuable evidence of existing disease problems. Any treatments undertaken should always be amply documented, particularly the concentrations of chemicals used and all the calculations involved, the duration of treatment, the time, date and sequel etc. Such records are necessary in order to compile an unique treatment schedule to advise the correct dosages for different conditions based upon experience in the particular farm under study. Table 5 gives a list of useful conversion factors for different units of weight, volume, flow rate etc.

3 Treatment methods
Fish are usually treated in one of three ways:
(i) adding chemicals to the water
(ii) adding chemicals to the feed
(iii) administering chemicals directly to individual fish.

(i) For treatment purposes, soluble chemicals are commonly added to the water in one of three different ways: as a dip, bath, or flush treatment. Most of the chemicals commonly used are themselves toxic to fish in some degree. Treatment always imposes stress on fish, which are already weakened anyway. In general, therefore, treatment should only be

Table 5 — Conversion factors

1 Weight

1 lb (16 oz)	= 454 g	1 ton	= 2240 lb
1 oz	= 28.4 g	1 metric ton	= 2204 lb
1 kg (1000 g)	= 2.2 lb (35.27 oz)		

2 Volume

1 gallon (8 pints or 4 quarts)	=	4.55 litres
1 litre (1000 cc or 1000 ml)	=	0.22 gallons
1 litre	=	1.76 pints (0.26 US gallons)
1 litre	=	35.2 fluid oz
1 cubic foot	=	28.3 litres
1 cubic foot	=	6.22 gallons
1 cubic yard	=	0.764 cu metre
1 cubic metre	=	1.308 cu yd
1 cubic metre	=	35.31 cu ft

3 Length

1 inch	= 25.4 mm (2.54 cm)
1 foot	= 30.48 cm
1 yard	= 0.914 m
1 metre	= 39.37 inches

4 Area

1 sq yd	= 0.836 sq metres
1 sq metre	= 1.196 sq yd
1 acre	= 4140 sq yd
1 hectare	= 2.47 acres

5 Water equivalent

1 gallon	= 10 lb (4.54 kg)
1 cu ft	= 6.23 gall (28.3 kg)

6 Flow rate

1 gallon per minute (gpm)	= 75.7 ml per sec = 75.7 cc per second
1 gallon per hour	= 1.26 ml per second
1 litre per second	= 13.2 gpm
1 cu ft per second	= 28.3 litre per sec (373.8 gpm)
1 cu ft per second	= 538,272 gall per day

7 Temperature

On the Centigrade scale, $0°C$ and $100°C$ represent the freezing and boiling points respectively of water (at standard pressure).
To convert Fahrenheit ($°F$) degrees to Centigrade ($°C$), use the formula:

$$°F = (°C \times \frac{9}{5}) + 32$$

NB
ppm = parts per million
1 ppm = 1 mg/litre = 1 : 1,000,000
1 g/litre = 1 : 1000 = 1000 ppm

147

undertaken after careful evaluation of the circumstances and must always be considered a necessary evil. A number of precautions must be taken whenever chemicals are added to the water for treatment purposes.

(a) Do not feed for 24 hours prior to the treatment.
(b) Use plastic buckets etc for mixing, and never use galvanized containers.
(c) Ensure that any calculations of dosage are based upon accurate waterflows and *usable* volumes of pond.
Have your arithmetic checked independently.
(d) Treat first thing in the morning or at minimal water temperatures.
(e) Always carry out an initial *trial* treatment with a few fish.
(f) Wait 12-24 hours after the trial treatment before carrying out the main treatment if the trial is successful.
(g) Watch the fish continuously during treatment and be ready to flush rapidly with fresh water, use aerators etc, should the fish become distressed.
(h) Only repeat the treatment if absolutely necessary and not within 30 hours of the first treatment.

For dip treatment, the solution is made up in a container into which a net containing the fish is dipped for a few seconds. For bath treatment, the water flow through a pond is stopped and the fish are bathed in the solution for a certain period of time; great care is needed to avoid killing the fish due to oxygen lack. Flush treatment involves adding the chemical to the inlet of a pond so that it runs through the system as a flush. In ponds with a high water exchange rate, *eg* raceways, where exposure to the drug is shorter, doses need to be higher (and therefore more critical). In certain systems, *eg* earth ponds, it is sometimes necessary to adopt a compromise between a bath and a flush.

(ii) Certain types of drug are best incorporated into the fish food as some diseases are only eliminated by this form of treatment. The main drawback with medicated food is that it is only effective if the fish are feeding normally, and many diseases will cause them to go off their food. Moreover, when pelleted foods are used, it is often difficult to persuade feed manufacturers to mix in the required drug during the manufacturing process. In this case, it is sometimes possible

148

for the farmer himself to make up a solution of the drug with gelatin water, and spray it onto the pellets before use (5% gelatin water used at a rate of 1 gallon/100 lb pellets).[2]

(iii) In the case of valuable fish, *eg* broodstock, it may be feasible for them to be treated individually. This will usually involve prior anaesthesia, and treatment might comprise procedures such as intramuscular injections, painting the skin with appropriate medicament, mechanical removal of large ectoparasites etc. Two examples of such treatments in adult salmon are the use of HCG (Human Chorionic Gonadotrophin) injections in spawnbound fish to facilitate stripping and the use of malachite green for painting large patches of skin fungus.

In the fish farming situation, the indications for this individual method of treatment are uncommon and in many countries injections may only be given under veterinary supervision. However, mass treatment of salmonid fish with drugs in the water and food is a regular practice and will therefore be discussed in more detail.

SPECIFIC TREATMENTS — (A) CHEMICALS ADDED TO THE WATER

(i) Copper sulphate.

Copper sulphate is sometimes used to treat external bacterial or parasitic infections, *eg* myxobacterial fin rot, columnaris disease.

It is particularly toxic to fish in waters which do not have high concentrations of dissolved salts, and should never be used unless the calcium content of the water is known.

In hard waters (>100ppm calcium), copper sulphate may be used as a one minute dip at a concentration of 1 : 2000 (500 ppm).

Copper sulphate may also be used as a flush treatment in tanks and raceways as follows:[3]

Water hardness (ppm of $CaCO_3$)	Concentration of flush
<50	Too toxic
50-100	⊁1 : 2,000,000 (⊁0.5 ppm)
100-200	⊁1 : 1,000,000 (⊁1 ppm)
200-400	⊁1 : 500,000 (⊁2 ppm)
>400	Ineffective

(NB ⊁ = *not* exceeding; < = less than; > = more than)

149

In raceways with hard water, one rule of thumb recommends 1 lb copper sulphate/2.5 cubic feet per second, *ie* 1 lb copper sulphate/935 gpm.

(ii) Formalin

Formalin is extremely useful for the treatment of external parasitic infections of skin and gills, especially *Costia* and other protozoans, and also monogenetic flukes.

Formalin is a 40% solution of formaldehyde, and care must be taken to ensure that it is not contaminated with paraformaldehyde, which forms a white precipitate at the bottom of the bottle and which is very toxic to fish.

Formalin has an irritant action on the respiratory membranes of humans as well as fish. It must therefore be handled with caution for personal safety and used with extreme care as a treatment. Where possible, microscopic evidence of parasitism should be obtained before treatment is undertaken and gills of treated fish should be examined before any further treatment is contemplated.

Formalin removes oxygen from solution and this effect reaches a peak approximately 24 hours after it has been added to a pond. If formalin cannot be completely eliminated from the water in a fish pond soon after treatment, then care should be taken to prevent oxygen deficiency occurring *eg* by using aerators.

When used as a bath, formalin should be thoroughly mixed into solution in order to achieve a final concentration of 1 : 5000 (200 ppm). It is often advisable to add a few drops of malachite green to the formalin initially, as the green dye will assist observation of adequate mixing throughout the pond. Under conditions of high water temperature, it may be advisable to use a concentration of 1 :6000 (167 ppm) and the duration of treatment should never exceed 1 hour. This is a common way of treating fish in raceways during which it is always advisable to bubble air or oxygen into the system continuously.

Because of the slow water exchange rate involved for treating fish in Danish-type earthponds, it is usually necessary to lower the water level and adopt a compromise between a bath and a flush. The pond is lowered to half its normal depth and the quantity of formalin calculated which will ensure a final concentration of 1 : 5000 (200 ppm) with the pond half full.[4] The required amount of formalin is mixed with water in a large plastic bucket and is slowly siphoned into the inlet monk over a period of 20 minutes. Throughout this period the water continues to flow through the pond and when all the formalin has been added, the pond is filled up again.

(iii) Formalin and malachite green

Formalin treatment will usually control white spot disease (Ich), but in certain stubborn outbreaks, a mixture of formalin and malachite green is more effective.

American workers[5] have obtained good results using 3.68 g of zinc-free malachite green per litre of formalin. This stock solution is then applied to yield a treatment concentration of 1 : 40,000 (25 ppm) by either of the methods proposed for formalin alone.

(iv) Furanace

This is the trade name of a nitrofuran derivative, nifurpirinol, which appears to have a broad spectrum of activity against pathogens of different families of fish including salmonids.

It will probably prove particularly effective against the bacterial diseases, *eg* various myxobacterial infections and vibriosis, but may also become increasingly used against certain parasitic conditions.

Because of its rapid absorption across gills and skin, Furanace may be used as a bath, and a concentration of 1 : 1,000,000 (1 ppm) for one hour is recommended.

(v) Hyamine 3500

Hyamine 3500 is a quaternary ammonium compound produced as a liquid, which is of particular value in treating bacterial gill disease among fry and fingerlings.

Toxicity of Hyamine to fish is markedly dependent upon the hardness of the water (*cf* copper sulphate).

In fry tanks the following concentrations may be used as a bath:

Water hardness (ppm of $CaCO_3$)	Concentration of bath
<100	1 : 500,000 (2 ppm)
100-200	1 : 330,000 (3 ppm)
>200	1 : 250,000 (4 ppm)

The chemical should be added slowly over the entire surface of the tank, and treatment should be for one hour, or less if the fish become in any way distressed.

For use in Danish-type earth ponds, it is necessary to lower the pond to half its normal depth (*cf* formalin). The quantity of Hyamine is calculated which will ensure a concentration of 1 : 500,000 (2 ppm) with the pond half full. This amount is then mixed in a plastic bucket and, to ensure careful mixing, one tenth of the total is mixed with a whole bucketful of water and poured into the inlet monk, and the process is repeated. After all ten bucketfuls of the drug have been used and the full dose administered, the pond is allowed to fill up again.

(vi) Malachite green

Malachite green is obtained as a crystalline solid which dissolves in water to give a green dye. It is important at purchase to stipulate that *zinc-free* malachite green is required in order to avoid lethal zinc toxicity problems (for the same reason, galvanized containers must always be avoided).

Malachite green is a very useful compound for treating fungus infections, particularly *Saprolegnia*. It is also of some value against White Spot disease (Ich).

As a dip treatment, malachite green may be used at a concentration of 1 : 15,000 (67 ppm) for a period not exceeding 30 seconds.

As a bath treatment, malachite green may be used at a concentration of 1 : 500,000 (2 ppm) for one hour for fry and fingerlings, and 1 : 1,000,000 (1 ppm) for one hour for adult fish.

For flush treatment in Danish-type earth ponds, a total dosage of 1 : 200,000 (5 ppm) is recommended. The required amount of malachite green is calculated and then is best added to the inlet monk over a period of approximately 2 hours (*eg* 5-6 tablespoonsful at the rate of ½ spoon every ten minutes).

Malachite green is highly valued as an antifungal agent for egg treatment. In this case a concentration of about 1 : 500,000 (2 ppm) is preferred for one hour. Since the waterflow cannot usually be stopped, this requires a continuous drip of the chemical which may be arranged using a constant flow siphon, or similar device.

(vii) Masoten

Masoten is the trade name of an organophosphorous compound, which is almost identical to Dipterex, Dylox, Neguvon etc.

This compound is of particular value against copepod ectoparasites, such as Fish Louse (*Argulus*), and Anchor worm (*Lernaea*) and also against Leeches; it will also kill some monogenetic flukes and *protozoa*. It is sprayed on large ponds or added to the inflow to achieve a total concentration of 1 : 4,000,000 (0.25 ppm) and allowed to dissipate out of the system. Two applications at an interval of one week are usually sufficient for large ectoparasites.

(viii) Anaesthetics

Anaesthetics are commonly used in order to immobilize fish for such procedures as stripping or injecting brood-stock.

Probably the most widely used anaesthetic for salmonids is methane tricainesulphonate, which is marketed under the trade name, MS 222. This is usually dissolved in water to give a final concentration within the range 1 : 25,000–1: 12,500 (40 ppm-80 ppm) and immobilization takes approximately 5 min. Less commonly concentrations of up to 1 : 5000 (200 ppm) are used to give more rapid immobilization. Recovery time is usually about 5 minutes and is reduced with an increase in water temperature.

Two other useful anaesthetics for salmonids are Quinaldine and Propoxate. Quinaldine is the trade name for 2-methyl-quinoline which is a liquid generally used at concentrations within the range 1 : 200,000–1 : 100,000 (5 ppm–10 ppm), although it does not very easily mix with water. Propoxate (R7464) is a solid and is effective at concentrations of 1 : 2,000,000–1 : 250,000 (0.5 ppm–4 ppm), salmon requiring a slightly higher dose than rainbow trout.

(ix) Miscellaneous chemical treatments

In certain cases of myxobacterial infection, *eg* Fin and Tail Rot, proflavine hemisulphate can be a useful bath treatment, at a concentration of 1 : 50,000 (20 ppm) for a period of 30 minutes.

Under conditions of oxygen deficiency, potassium permanganate ($KMnO_4$) can be of value in reducing BOD of the water (*eg* following formalin treatment of a heavily stocked pond in mid-summer).[6] Addition of potassium permanganate to give a concentration in the pond of 1 : 1,000,000–1 : 500,000 (1 ppm–2 ppm.) is sometimes a useful contingency measure during installation of aerators, pumps etc.

Frescon is the trade name for the molluscicide, *n*-tritylmorpholine, which has been used to kill the lymnaeid snails acting as intermediate hosts for Eye fluke. In a reservoir trial, a concentration of 0.025 ppm was successful in killing the snails without causing trout mortalities. Regular treatments would probably be required and it is emphasized that the safety margin is likely to be too low for use in fish farms at the present time.

Various other chemicals, *eg* methylene blue, are used on certain trout and salmon farms, but are not described here as it is considered that they are probably inferior in effectiveness and safety to those already considered.

Specimen calculations:

1 Malachite green as an antifungal treatment for eggs:

It is required to treat a series of hatchery trays with malachite green at a concentration of 1 : 500,000 (2 ppm) for one hour using a constant flow siphon.

- (a) ascertain flow rate = *eg* 4 gpm
- (b) calculate hourly flow rate = 4 × 60 = 240 gphour
- (c) convert to millilitres = 240 × 4.55 × 1000 = 1,092,000 ml
- (d) calculate weight of malachite green for required concentration

$$= \frac{1,092,000}{500,000} = 2.18 \text{ g.}$$

So it is necessary to dissolve 2.18 g of malachite green in one gallon of water within the siphon bottle. When the siphon is set in operation this will give a 1 : 500,000 (2 ppm) concentration of malachite green in a 4 gpm inflow over a period of 1 hour.

2 Hyamine 3500 as a myxobacterial treatment in Danish-type earth ponds:

It is required to treat a pond of fingerlings suffering from bacterial gill disease with Hyamine.

- (a) ascertain hardness of water = *eg* 80 ppm $CaCO_3$.
- (b) compute required concentration of Hyamine = 2 ppm for one hour.

(c) calculate volume of pond when half-full only = *eg*
    100′ × 30′ × 1.5′ = 4500 cubic feet.
(d) calculate volume of pond (half-full) in millilitres
    = 4500 × 28,300 = 127,350,000 ml.
(e) calculate volume of Hyamine for required concentration

$$= \frac{127,350,000 \times 2}{1,000,000} = 254.7 \text{ ml.}$$

So 255 ml of Hyamine are poured into the inlet monk diluted in water to give ten bucketfuls of solution. The water level is then raised to the normal height once again.

3 Formalin treatment in raceways:
It is required to bathe growers for ectoparasitic infection in raceways, using a concentration of 1 : 5000 (200 ppm) for one hour, with appropriate aeration facilities.

(a) ascertain treatment depth from weight of fish present
    (*eg* 1500 lb) = 3 × 6 = 18″
(b) ascertain treatment volume of raceway = *eg*
    100′ × 8′ × 1.5′ = 1200 cubic feet.
(c) convert to gallons = 1200 × 6.22 = 7464 gallons.
(d) calculate volume of formalin to give required concentration = 7464/5000 = 1.49 gallons.
Therefore 1.49 gallons of formalin have to be carefully spread and thoroughly mixed over the entire length of the raceway (preferably using a little malachite green dye to allow visible evidence of mixing) to give a 1 : 5000 concentration at a depth of 1½ ft for one hour.

NB In order to calculate the weight of a chemical required to give a particular dilution in a known volume of water, the following formula may be used.
WEIGHT (grams) = 4546 × DILUTION (as a fraction) × VOLUME (gallons)
Thus, in specimen calculation no 1 above, the required weight of malachite green

$$= 4546 \times \frac{1}{500,000} \times 240 = 2.18 \text{ g.}$$

SPECIFIC TREATMENTS — (B) DRUGS ADDED TO THE FEED

1. di-*n*-butyl tin oxide
This compound is a solid which has been reported of some value in treating thorny-headed worms (acanthocephalans) and fish tapeworms (cestodes) occurring in the gut (*ie* excluding *Diphyllobothrium* spp.)

The usual dosage rate is 11.34 g/100 lb of fish, or as 0.3% of feed levels per day, for a period of 5 days.

2 Enheptin
Enheptin is the trade name of 2-amino 5-nitrothiazole, also called Acinitrasole. It is widely used for the treatment of *Octomitus (Hexamita)* infection of the gut and the usual dosage rate is 2 g/100 lb of fish per day for 5 days.

An alternative treatment for *Octomitus* at some American hatcheries[7] is Epsom salts (magnesium sulphate) given as 3% of feed levels. Calomel (mercurous chloride) and Carbarsone (an arsenical) were formerly used widely but tend to be unsafe to fish handler and to consumer. More recently, with the difficulties sometimes experienced in obtaining Enheptin and Carbarsone, Furazolidone has been used with success (see below).

3 Antibacterial treatments
Bacterial septicaemias, notably furunculosis but also vibrosis etc, are usually sensitive to a variety of different antibiotics, sulphonamides and nitrofurans. Many of these drugs are used in human medicine and because of the danger associated with drug resistance and the possible transfer of such resistance from fish to humans, it is vital that they should not be used indiscriminately. Some drugs, *eg* chloramphenicol, should never be used with fish destined for human consumption. It is important to give a proper course of treatment with antibacterial compounds, and not to use them at low levels as this will encourage the development of drug-resistant strains of bacteria. For acute bacterial infections in salmonids, of the various drugs available, sulphamerazine, furazolidone and oxytetracycline are recommended *in that order*. Table 6 should be consulted to enable rapid calculation of the amount of the drug to be mixed in with a particular

Table 6 Medicated Food — Calculation Table
How much of each drug to add to 100 lb of feed (g)

Feeding rate %	Dosage level g/100 lb of feed						
	Enheptin	Oxytetracycline pure	Furazolidone pure	Sulphamerazine pure	di-n-butyl tin oxide	Neftin — Furazolidone supplement	Terramedic — Oxytetracycline supplement
0.5	400	700	1000	2000	2268	4400	5200
1.0	200	350	500	1000	1134	2200	2600
1.5	133	233	333	667	680	1470	1733
2.0	100	175	250	500	567	1100	1300
2.5	80	140	200	400	454	880	1040
3.0	67	117	167	333	340	733	866
3.5	57	100	143	286	324	628	743
4.0	50	88	125	250	284	550	650
4.5	45	78	111	222	252	490	578
5.0	40	70	100	200	227	440	520
5.5	36	64	91	182	206	400	473
6.0	33	58	83	167	170	367	433

proportion of food.[8] As indicated above, Furazolidone is also now used in *Octomitis* parasite infections.

(i) Sulphamerazine

Sulphamerazine is probably the drug of choice in most instances and several different dosage regimes have been recommended. In severe infections a loading dose of 10 g/100 lb of fish should be given on the first day and thereafter 5 g/100 lb fish per day for at least 10 days. A suitable alternative dose for milder outbreaks is 9 g/100 lb daily for 3 days followed by 2 days without treatment and then 2 more days each at 9 g/100 lb of fish. Sulphamerazine is best avoided in brown trout as it may retard growth of this species.

(ii) Furazolidone

It is available as 'Neftin supplement' in the United Kingdom. Neftin contains 100 g furazolidone per pound of supplement. The recommended dosage of pure furazolidone is 5 g/100 lb fish/day which is equivalent to 22 g Neftin/100 lb fish/day. Treatment should be for 5-10 days. Note that furazolidone is rapidly decomposed when added to moist diets and thus it should be fed to fish immediately after being added to such diets.

(iii) Oxytetracycline

It is available as 'Terramedic Powder' (poultry formula) in the United Kingdom. Terramedic contains 60 g oxytetracycline per pound of powder. The recommended dosage cf pure oxytetracycline is 3.5 g/100 lb fish/day which is equivalent to 26 g Terramedic/100 lb fish/day. Treatment should be for 5-10 days.

PRECAUTIONS

1 It must always be borne in mind that in most countries (including the UK) antibiotics and other antimicrobial drugs used in human medicine may only be obtained on a veterinary prescription.

2 To prevent the possibility of anybody eating these drugs, fish which have been under treatment should not be slaughtered (or planted out) until at least 3 weeks after the drug was last administered.

3 The most critical calculation is the feeding rate. When you

prepare the medicated food the feeding rate determines, at a given dose, how much drug goes into the diet. If you assume a feeding rate of 3% and the fish only eat 1.5%, they only get half the correct dose. So make sure you get it right!

Specimen calculation
1 Decide the dosage and length of treatment. These are recommended in the text.
2 Choose a feeding rate 0.5% lower than the one you have been using, *ie* normal feeding rate 3%, medicated diet feeding rate 2.5%.
3 Find out the total weight of fish requiring treatment.
4 Work out how much food you will need for the length of treatment, *ie* 450 lb of fish, feeding rate 2.5% for 10 days. Food required

$$= 450 \times \frac{2.5}{100} \times 10 = 112.5 \text{ lb, say } 120 \text{ lb.}$$

5 Turn to table 6 on page 157. This will tell you how much drug to add to 100 lb of feed for your particular dosage and feeding rate, *ie*.

Sulphamerazine 5 g/100 lb fish at 2.5%
You need 200 g for 100 lb feed.
However, you require 120 lb feed, so you need to add

$$200 \times \frac{120}{100} = 240 \text{ g.}$$

Appendices

A THE MICROSCOPE ON THE FISH FARM

A microscope is a very expensive precision instrument which can only be used correctly if the basic structure and function is understood.

Microscopes should always be covered when not in use, either in a case or by a waterproof, dustproof cover.

The diagram (Fig 76) shows the parts of a standard microscope with a built-in light source. Many older microscopes have a mirror for purposes of illumination.

Microscopes are available in many price ranges. You get what you pay for, and good lenses are very expensive. A new microscope with built-in light source, suitable for fish farm work, cannot be bought for less than £200 (approx $400). Good second-hand microscopes are sometimes available from medical students and older brass ones with good lenses can be excellent, but inexpensive modern microscopes are not to be recommended. Eyepieces should be 10× and the objectives most used are 10× and 40× giving total magnification of 100× and 400× respectively. Since a microscope on a fish farm is often used for examining wet mounts of material containing moving specimens, a moving stage, which can be readily manipulated, is highly recommended.

Use of the microscope

The stand should be placed on a firm surface with a light source such as the sun, or a torch, or electric bulb available if the microscope is not supplied with a light built in. The light should be switched on and mirror focussed as necessary.

The slide to be examined is placed between the clips on the viewing stage or between the arms of the moving stage. The appropriate objective lens is swung into position and the condenser (if fitted) focussed by means of the condenser control knob, to allow good illumination.

Fig 76 Post-mortem equipment required on the fish farm. The microscope must be capable of magnification up to 400x and built-in light and moveable stage are of great advantage.

Focussing

Turn the coarse adjustment knob, *whilst watching the slide and objective, not looking down the microscope,* until the objective is about ½ cm from the specimen, then look down the eyepiece and turn the coarse adjustment knob until the specimen comes roughly into focus. Then it should be brought into perfect focus with the fine adjustment. Because the 40× lens has a depth of focus only one fifth that of the 10× objective, it is not possible to extract the maximum amount of information from a specimen using the 40× objective unless the fine focus control is constantly moved up and down through the planes of focus.

Care of lenses

The lenses are the most expensive and fragile parts of a microscope and should be treated with the utmost care. If they become dirty they should be cleaned with a special lens cleaning tissue, ideally dipped in a little xylene. Do not use methylated spirits or acetone to clean lenses as these may damage the lens cement.

B USEFUL REFERENCES

1 Amlacher, E (1970). Textbook of fish diseases — English translation by D A Conroy and R L Herman. T F H Publications. 302 pp.

2 Bureau of Sport Fisheries and Wildlife, US Dept of the Interior, Fish and Wildlife Service/Division of Fishery Research, Washington, DC 20240 — various publications are recommended, in particular:
(i) 'The Progressive Fish-Culturist' (a quarterly periodical for fishery biologists and fish-culturists).
(ii) A series of 'Fish Disease Leaflets' (each on a specific topic).
(iii) 'Progress in Sport Fishery Research' (an annual review).

3 Davis, H S (1956). Culture and diseases of game fishes. Berkeley, Univ of California Press. 332 pp.

4 Halver, J E (Ed) (1972). Fish nutrition. New York and London, Academic Press. 713 pp.

5 Hoffman, G L and Meyer, F P (1974). Parasites of freshwater fishes. T F H Publications. 224 pp.

6 Leitritz, E (1969). Trout and salmon culture (hatchery methods). Fish Bull No 107 Dept of Fish and Game, State of California, 169 pp.

7 Roberts, R J (Ed) (1978). Fish Pathology. London, Bailliere Tindall. 318 pp.

8 Sarig, S (1971). Diseases of Fishes: Book III, The prevention and treatment of diseases of warm-water fishes under subtropical conditions, with special emphasis on intensive fish farming. T F H Publications, 127 pp.

9 Snieszko, S F, Bullock, G L and others (1971). Diseases of Fishes: Book II, Bacterial diseases. T F H Publications. 150 pp.

10 Wedemeyer, G A, Meyers, F P and Smith, L (1976). Disease of Fishes: Book V, Environmental stress and fish diseases. TFH Publications.

11 Wood, J W (1968). Diseases of Pacific salmon, their prevention and treatment. Dept of Fisheries, Hatchery Division, Olympia, State of Washington. 73 pp.

C USEFUL DRUGS AND CHEMICALS

This list of drugs and chemicals is useful for the treatment of fish. It gives their main indications, and their manufacturers or the main UK suppliers.

Table 7 Trout Diseases — Useful Drugs and Chemicals

Trade Name	Chemical Name (or generic name)	Main indication	Manufacturer and/ or UK supplier
Butyl Tin Oxide	di-n-butyl tin oxide	Tapeworms	British Drug Houses
Enheptin (Acinitrasole)	2-amino 5-nitrothiazole	*Hexamila (Octomitus)*	Aldrich Chem. Co. (Gillingham, Dorset)
FAM (Vanodine Fam)	'Iodophor'	Disinfection	Vanodine International (Eccles)
Frescon	n-trityl-morpholine	Snails (Eye Fluke)	Shell Chemicals
Furanace	Nifurpirinol	Bacterial septicaemias etc.	Dainippon Pharmaceuticals; Piscisan (Enfield)
Hyamine 3500	'Quaternary ammonium compound'	Bacterial Gill Disease	Rohm & Haas (UK) (Ltd) (Croydon)
Masoten (*cf* Dipterex, Dylox, Neguvon etc.)	'Organo-phosphorous compound'	Ectoparasites (esp *Crustacea*)	Bayer Agrochemicals
MS 222	Tricaine methane sulphonate	Anaesthesia	Thomson & Joseph (Norwich)
Neftin	Furazolidone	Bacterial septicaemias	Smith, Kline & French
Propoxate	'R 7464'	Anaesthesia	Janssen Pharmaceutica
Quinaldine	2-methylquinoline	Anaesthesia	Aldrich Chem. Co. (Gillingham, Dorset)
Sulphamerazine	────────→	Bacterial septicaemias	May & Baker
Terramedic	Oxytetracycline	Bacterial septicaemias	Pfizer
Wescodyne	'Iodophor'	Disinfection	Ciba-Geigy

NB Common proprietary chemicals, *eg* formalin, may be purchased from most chemical wholesale companies.

Index

Acanthocephalans, 44, 54, 143, 144
Achtheres, 44, 57
Adrenal, 22, 33
Aeromonas, 69, 102, 132, 134
   Aeromonas salmonicida, 101,
   Autumn aeromonad, 102, 134
Aflatoxins, 128
A. hydrophila, 68, 69, 134
Anaemia, 125, 142
Anaesthetics, 149, 153, 164
Anchor-worm — *Learnea*, 44, 56, 57, 58, 107, 153
Anisakis, 44, 57, 60, 141
Anus, 23, 30, 78
Argulus — see Fish Louse
A. salmonicida, see Furunculosis

Bacterial diseases, 67, 68, 69, 70, 71, 100, 118, 136, 138, 140, 151, 154
Bacterial gill disease, 70, 91, 92, 126
Bacterial kidney disease (BKD), 94, 114, 115, 116, 119, 120 ,
Bacterial septicaemias, 94, 95, 102, 156
Bald spots, 140
Black Spot — *Cryptocotyle*, 44, 62, 63, 120
Bladder, 22, 30
Blue-sac disease, 83, 84
Botulism, 102, 106, 124, 128
Bouins Fluid, 130
Brain, 22, 31, 33
Broodstock, diseases of, 131-143
Butyl tin oxide, 116, 142, 156, 159, 164

Cancer, see Tumour
Ceratomyxa, 44, 45

Char, 20
   European, 20, 21
Chilodonella, 44, 52, 53
Chronic diseases, 111, 112, 113-116
Circulatory system, 22, 27, 28
Clostridium botulinum, 102, 128
Coarse fish, 20
Coldwater disease — *Cytophaga* spp., 70, 71, 121, 122
Columnaris disease, *Flexibacter columnaris*, 70, 71, 138
Copper sulphate, 92, 111, 149, 150
Coregonini, 17, 20, 21
Corpuscles of Stannius, 33
Corynebacteria, 69, 119, 132
Costia, 44, 45, 46, 47, 52, 86, 90, 91, 92, 94, 95, 106, 107, 110
Cotylurus, 44, 63
Crustaceans, 44, 56, 57
Cryptocaryon, 51
Cryptocotyle, 44, 62, 63, 120
Cytophaga, 68, 70, 71
Cystidicola, 44, 60, 142

Dactylogyrus, 44, 61, 62, 110
Diagnosis, 76-80
Dieldrin, 130
Diet infections — see food
Digestive system, 22, 28
Dinoflagellates, 73
Diphyllobothrium, 44, 55, 142, 164, 156
Diplostomum — see Eye Fluke
Diplozoon, 44, 62
Dipterex, see Masoten
Discocotyle, 44, 62
Dolly Varden, 20, 21
Dylox, see Masoten

Endocrine system, 22, 33
Enheptin, 91, 105, 156, 157, 164
Epidermis, 22, 23
Ergasilus, 44, 57
Eroded mouth, 70
Eubothrium, 44, 54, 56, 142
Excretory system, 22, 30
Eye sight, 31, 32, 62, 64, 65, 78,
    105, 125, 126, 140
Eye fluke — *Diplostomum*, 44,
    64, 65, 78, 94, 111, 112, 140

Fam, 145, 164
Farming, 36, 40, 76, 77, 81, 82,
    83, 84, 86, 90, 130
    Marine, 37, 117, 122
Fat diseases, 127
Filariid worms, 44, 60, 142
Fin, 24, 77, 108, 109
    Adipose, 20, 21, 23, 26, 52
    Anal, 23
    Dorsal, 20, 23
    Pelvic, 23
    Ventral, 20
Fin rot, 70, 94, 95, 108, 109,
    111, 115
Fish kills, 81, 89, 94, 95, 97, 118,
    129, 130, 131, 145
Fish-louse — *Argulus*, 44, 56, 58,
    107, 141, 153
Flashing, 76, 92, 96, 104, 105,
    106, 107, 120
Flexibacter columnaris, 68, 69,
    70, 71, 136
Fluke — Digenetic, 44, 63, 64
    Monogenetic, 44, 61, 62, 120,
        140, 150, 153
    See also — Eye fluke
Food, 38, 76
    Diet infection, 87-93, 122
    Treatment administered via
        food, 146, 148, 156, 157,
        158, 159
Formalin, 81, 86, 91, 93, 105,
    107, 110, 120, 130, 150, 151,
    153, 155, 164
Frescon, 111, 154, 164
Fungal diseases, 73, 74, 75, 134,
    140
    Saprolegnia, 136, 152
Fungi, 39, 94, 95

Furanace, 151, 164
Furazolidone, 156, 157, 158
Furunculosis, 69, 101, 108, 138,
    156

Gall bladder, 29, 50, 91
Gas bubble disease, 84, 85, 86,
    88, 97
Gill, 26, 27, 35, 36, 37, 46, 52,
    57, 59, 62, 67, 77, 78, 85,
    86, 90, 91, 92, 94, 95, 98,
    105, 126, 127, 140, 140,
    151, 154
    Bacterial disease of — see
        Bacterial gill disease
Gill fungus, 91, 92
Gill maggot — *Salmincola*, 44, 57,
    59, 140, 141
Glochidia, 44, 67
Goblet cells, 22
Grading, 40
Grayling, 20, 21
Grilse, 17, 21, 25
Growers, 96, 100
Gwynniad, 17
Gyrodactylus, 44, 61, 62, 106,
    107, 120

Haemophilus piscium, 68, 69
Haemorrhage, 35, 119, 127, 132,
    134, 138, 141, 142, 143
Hatching, 40, 81, 82, 83, 84
Heart, 23, 27, 63
Henneguya, 44, 45, 48, 142
Herring — freshwater, 17
Hexamita, 50, 51, 80, 91, 93, 94,
    95, 103, 105, 115, 156
Hormone, 22, 24, 31, 33, 132
Husbandry, 34, 76, 91, 93, 108,
    109, 115, 118
Hyamine, 92, 110, 151, 152, 154,
    155, 164

Ichthyophonus, 73, 74, 123
Ichthyophthirius — see White spot
Ichtyobodo, see *Costia*
Incubation, 40
Infectious diseases, 43, 131, 132
Infectious haematopoietic necro-
    sis (IHN), 72, 73, 90, 94, 95,
    100, 101

Infectious pancreatic necrosis (IPN), 72, 89, 90, 94, 95, 100, 101, 105, 111
Integumentary system, 22
Intestine, 22, 23, 28, 29, 50
Iodophors, 90, 130, 144, 145

Kelts, 140
Kidney, 22, 23, 28, 30, 33, 69, 80, 98, 99, 115, 118, 119, 123, 132, 138
    See also — Bacterial kidney disease
    Corynebacteria
Krill, 57

Lamprey, 44, 65, 66
Lateral line, 20, 21, 23
Leeches, 44, 65, 66, 67, 153
Lernaea — See Anchor worm
Lepeophtheirus, 44, 57, 59, 120, 121, 141
Liver, 23, 29, 80, 98, 123, 127, 128, 132, 141, 143

Malachite Green, 39, 81, 92, 105, 107, 135, 149, 152, 154, 155
Malnutrition, 124
Masoten, 107, 152, 153, 164
Metazoans, 44, 52
Milky-flesh disease — *Henneguya*, 44, 45, 48, 142
Microscope, 160-162
Mineral and trace element diseases, 126, 127
MS 222, see Anaesthetics
Mucus, 22
Muscular system, 22, 125
Mussel glochidia, 44, 67
Mycobacteria, 68, 69, 70, 113, 114, 122, 123
Myxobacteria, 70, 71, 120, 122, 153
Myxosoma, 44, 48, 50, 103, 104

Neftin, 157, 158
Neguvon, see Masoten
Nematodes, 44, 57, 60
Nephrocalcinosis, 115
Nervous system, 22, 31

Nocardia, 68, 69, 70, 96, 97, 113, 122, 123
Nutritional diseases, 124, 126, 128

Octomitus, see *Hexamita*
Olfactory organ, 31, 32
Oncorhynchus, 17, 18, 21
Oodinium, 44, 51, 52
Operculum, 23, 26, 33, 138
Optic lobes, 31, 32
Oregon Sockeye disease (OSD), 72
    See also Infectious haematopoietic necrosis
Organochlorides, 130
Organophosphorous compounds, 130
Ovary, 22, 31
Oxytetracycline, 102, 156, 157, 158, 164
.

Pancreas, 23, 29, 72
Pantothenic acid, 126
Parasitic diseases, 43, 44, 45, 46, 47, 48, 49, 50, 51-67, 77, 78, 90, 92, 93, 102, 103, 105, 120, 121, 122, 140-143, 144, 150, 153, 155
Parr, 17, 18, 20, 120
Peduncle disease — *Cytophaga* spp., 70, 109, 110
Pike, 55, 56, 143
Pituitary, 22, 33
Plistophora, 44, 51
Poisoning, 130
Pollan, 17
Post-mortem, 77, 78, 130, 161
Potassium permanganate, 153, 154
Powan, 17, 21
Prevention of disease, 144-146
Proflavine hemisulphate, 153
Proliferative kidney disease (PKD), 94, 115, 116
Propoxate, see Anaesthetics
Protozoa, 44, 45, 140, 142, 150, 153
Pseudomonas fluorescens, 68, 69, 102
Pyridoxine, 126

Quinaldine, see Anaesthetics

Redmouth — *Enterobacteria*, 69
'Red Tide', 73
Reproductive system, 22, 31
Respiratory system, 22, 26
Riboflavin, 126

Sac-fry — Alevins, 83, 84, 85, 86
Sacramento River Chinook disease (SRCD), 72
   See also Infectious haematopoietic necrosis
Salmincola, see Gill Maggot
Salmon,
   Atlantic, 17, 18, 21, 25, 27, 32, 37, 46, 47, 57, 85, 87, 88, 101, 106, 114, 121, 124, 132, 136, 140
   Blue-back, 19
   Chinook or King, 19, 21, 122
   Chum, 19, 21
   Coho, 19, 21, 48, 122
   Japanese, 19, 21
   Kokanee, 19
   Land-locked, 18, 19
   Pacific, 17, 18, 72, 90, 113, 114, 115, 138
   Pink, 19, 21
   Sockeye, 19, 21, 70
Salmo, 17, 21
Salmon Louse — *Lepeophtheirus*, 44, 57, 59
Salmonidae, 17, 20, 21
Salmonini, 17, 20, 21
Salmon Parr, 76
Salmon pox, 72, 108, 121, 140
Salvelinus, 20, 21
Saprolegnia, 73, 74, 75, 82, 133, 134
Scales, 18, 20, 21, 22, 24, 25
Scolecobasidium, 75
Scyphidia, 44, 51, 93, 106
Sea lice — *Lepeophtheirus*, 120, 121, 141
Seawater precocity, 70
Skin, 24, 32, 45, 48, 52, 53, 62, 68, 71, 72, 77, 86, 98, 102, 103, 104, 105, 106, 107, 108, 109, 120, 121, 122, 129, 132, 135, 138, 139, 140
Smolt, 17

Spawning, 39
Spinal cord, 22, 32
Spine, 24
Spleen, 23, 30, 123, 132
Starvation, 88
Steelhead, 18, 21
Streptomyces, 70
Sulphamerazine, 102, 157, 158, 159, 160, 164
Swim bladder, 29, 30, 60, 96, 98

Table production, 17, 18, 19, 20
Tapeworms — Cestodes, 44, 54, 55, 115, 142, 143, 156
   Diphyllobothrium latum, 142
   Eubothrium, 142
Terramedic, 157, 158, 164
Testis, 22, 31, 98
Thiamine, 125, 126
Thorney-headed worms — *Acanthocephalans*, 44, 54, 115, 142, 143, 156
Thymallus, 20, 21,
Thymus gland, 138, 139
Thyroid, 33
Treatments, 146-159, 164
   Malachite green, 135, 137, 149,150, 151, 152, 154, 155
   di-*n*-butyl tin oxide, 142, 156
   Copper sulphate, 149, 150
   Formalin, 150-151, 155
   Furanace, 151
   Hyamine 3500, 151, 154, 155
   Masoten, 152-153
   Anaesthetics, 153
   Other specific treatments, 153, 154, 156
Triaenophorus, 44, 55, 56, 143
Trichodina, 52, 93, 94, 95, 106
Trichodinella, 52
Trout,
   Brook, 17, 20, 21, 76, 140
   Brown, 17, 18, 20, 21, 76, 97, 102, 133, 135, 158
   Cut-throat, 21
   Lake, 20, 21
   Rainbow, 17, 18, 20, 21, 26, 37, 40, 48, 64, 65, 67, 69, 72, 76, 84, 85, 90, 97, 102, 103, 104, 112, 135, 140

Trout — *cont.*
  Sea, 17, 18, 21, 45, 57, 137, 141
Tuberculosis — *Mycobacteria*, 69, 70, 113, 122, 123
Tumours, 138, 139
  Skin, 135

Ulcer, 135, 138
Ulcer disease — *Haemophilus*, 69
Ulcerative dermal necrosis (UDN), 135, 136, 137, 138
Ureter, 23
Urogenital papilla, 23

Vendace, 17
Vibrio anguillarum, 71, 118, 119, 138, 151, 156
Viral haemorrhagic septicaemia (VHS), 73, 97, 98, 99, 100, 111

Virus diseases, 71, 72, 73, 80, 89, 91, 96, 97, 130, 140, 144
Visceral Granuloma/nephrocalcinosis, 115
Vitamin diseases, 124, 125, 126
Vomer, 20

Wescodyne, 144, 164
White spot (Ich) — *Ichthyophthirius*, 44, 45, 48, 49, 94, 95, 103, 104, 105, 106, 107, 141, 151, 152
Wild fish, diseases of, 131-143
Whirling disease — *Myxosoma*, 40, 45, 48, 50, 77, 94, 95, 96, 103, 104, 111, 145
Whitefish, 17, 20

Yolk sac, 82, 83, 84, 85, 86, 87

Other books published by Fishing News Books Limited Farnham, Surrey, England

Free catalogue available on request

A living from lobsters
Advances in aquaculture
Aquaculture practices in Taiwan
Better angling with simple science
British freshwater fishes
Coastal aquaculture in the Indo-Pacific region
Commercial fishing methods
Control of fish quality
Culture of bivalve molluscs
Eel capture, culture, processing and marketing
Eel culture
European inland water fish: a multilingual catalogue
FAO catalogue of fishing gear designs
FAO catalogue of small scale fishing gear
FAO investigates ferro-cement fishing craft
Farming the edge of the sea
Fish and shellfish farming in coastal waters
Fish catching methods of the world
Fish farming international No 2
Fish inspection and quality control
Fisheries oceanography
Fishery products
Fishing boats and their equipment
Fishing boats of the world 1
Fishing boats of the world 2
Fishing boats of the world 3
Fishing ports and markets
Fishing with electricity
Fishing with light
Freezing and irradiation of fish
Handy medical guide for seafarers
How to make and set nets
Inshore fishing: its skills, risks, rewards
International regulation of marine fisheries: a study of regional fisheries
     organizations
Marine pollution and sea life
Mechanization of small fishing craft
Mending of fishing nets
Modern deep sea trawling gear
Modern fishing gear of the world 1
Modern fishing gear of the world 2
Modern fishing gear of the world 3
Modern inshore fishing gear
More Scottish fishing craft and their work
Multilingual dictionary of fish and fish products

Navigation primer for fishermen
Netting materials for fishing gear
Pair trawling and pair seining — the technology of two boat fishing
Pelagic and semi-pelagic trawling gear
Planning of aquaculture development — an introductory guide
Power transmission and automation for ships and submersibles
Refrigeration on fishing vessels
Salmon and trout farming in Norway
Salmon fisheries of Scotland
Seafood fishing for amateur and professional
Ships' gear 66
Sonar in fisheries: a forward look
Stability and trim of fishing vessels
Testing the freshness of frozen fish
Textbook of fish culture; breeding and cultivation of fish
The fertile sea
The fish resources of the ocean
The fishing cadet's handbook
The lemon sole
The marketing of shellfish
The seine net: its origin, evolution and use
The stern trawler
The stocks of whales
Training fishermen at sea
Trawlermen's handbook
Tuna: distribution and migration
Underwater observation using sonar